CUTTING MACHINE CRAFTS

CRICUT®, SIZZIX®, or SILHOUETTE®

Projects to Make with 60 SVG Files

LIA GRIFFITH

CLARKSON POTTER/PUBLISHERS
NEW YORK

TO MY AMAZING TEAM
*Your individual creativity
inspires me everyday!*

Published in the United States by Clarkson Potter/Publishers, an imprint of the
Crown Publishing Group, a division of Penguin Random House LLC, New York.
crownpublishing.com
clarksonpotter.com

CLARKSON POTTER is a trademark and POTTER with colophon is a registered
trademark of Penguin Random House LLC.

Library of Congress Cataloging-in-Publication Data is available upon request.

ISBN 978-1-984-82235-2
Ebook ISBN 978-1-984-82236-9

Printed in the United States of America

Book design by Deanna Washington
Interior and cover photography by Brian McDonnell
Photo styling: Anna Sjoberg-Smith and Lia Griffith
Cover design by Mia Johnson

10 9 8 7 6 5 4 3 2 1

First Edition

contents

FOR THE HOME

FOR THE KIDS

FOR CELEBRATIONS

It was five years ago when I loudly claimed, "The electronic cutting machine has changed my life!" Little did I know how true that bold statement would become. As a craft and lifestyle designer, I quickly understood how this machine could help me design three-dimensional projects like my paper flowers in a whole new way; it also added new possibilities by allowing me to cut out designs on iron-on transfers and vinyl. This die-cutting machine felt as essential to my crafting as a laser printer is to writing. Now in our growing design studio you'll see a machine on every designer's desk, and the buzz of the cutting throughout the day has become part of our creative environment.

There are so many things I love about this new craft tool. Not only does it speed up project preparation and ease the prototyping of new designs, it's also allowed me to personalize, style, decorate, and design my entire life. I've now DIY'd my own home decor, added motifs and monograms to electronics and gear, crafted personalized gifts, set gorgeous tables for entertaining, decorated for every holiday of the year, made custom t-shirts . . . I could go on!

The practice of hand-making, of infusing personality into the process of creating, has brought me satisfaction and joy throughout my life. And I'm excited to share that passion with you through these pages, so that you, too, can experience the joy of that hand-to-heart connection. Join me as we craft together. Perhaps you'll find that a personal cutting machine could change your life as well.

Lia

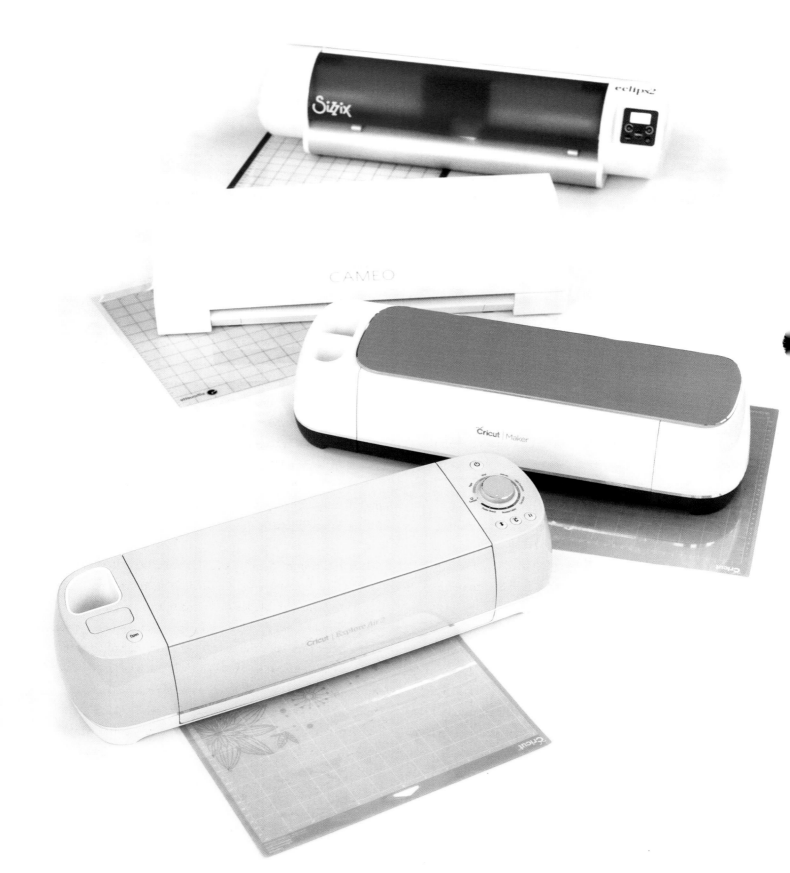

the electronic cutting machine

There are many different electronic cutting machines on the market and from my research and experience Cricut, Silhouette, and Sizzix are leading the pack. The machine you choose will depend on your personal preference but for these three brands my model recommendations include: Cricut Explore Air, Cricut Maker, Silhouette Cameo, and Sizzix Eclips2.

For paper, vinyl, and iron-on materials, all of these machines offer flexibility for both the beginner and advanced crafters. If you are still deciding on a machine, you can make most of these projects with sharp scissors, or a craft knife and cutting mat (some of the more complicated designs might be difficult to cut by hand). Simply use the printable PDF templates that you can download with the project files (see Project Templates on page 12).

WHICH MACHINE IS RIGHT FOR YOU?

You'll find a few different kinds of electronic cutting machines for sale. Many of them include similar features and new models debut every year. Here are my favorite machines; be sure to do your research to find the one that's right for you:

Cricut Explore has been the machine used in our studio for the past few years. It offers a dual head for you to insert a scoring tool or pen tool beside the cutting blade. The machine holds a standard and deep cut blade. Cricut's new machines operate with their Design Space software where you can use their library of cut files, download your Cricut cartridges into My Projects in the software, or upload your own files. Cricut offers a broad variety of paper, vinyl, and other cutting materials that work well with this machine. This machine will also cut bonded fabrics and heavier materials with a multiple cut setting.

Cricut Maker is the newest model in the Cricut family. It also offers a dual head for a scoring and pen tool but the biggest feature on the Maker is the variety of blades available. The new rotary cutter will cut fabric, felt, and crepe paper with exquisite perfection and the new knife blade offers thick material options. The Maker uses the Design Space software, making this machine an easy upgrade if you are familiar with the Explore.

Sizzix Eclips2 is another solid machine and has the fastest cutting ability of the machines listed. Its single head allows you to change to a pen holder. The machine's setting offers a score option that uses the same cutting blade. Though it does not cut heavier materials as well as the Cricut, it is great machine for paper, vinyl, heat transfer and bonded fabrics. The Eclips2 comes with the software eCal lite and is compatible with the SCAL software. You can choose from their library of designs or upload your own into the software for successful projects.

Silhouette Cameo 3 has a loyal following as Silhouette has a history of creating good products. This newest machine has a dual head for blades and pens but will require a workaround for solid scoring on paper. Simply change your blade setting on both the machine and in the software to the lightest cut for the score lines. Silhouette has a standard and deep cut blade for thicker materials and is the only machine that can cut a full roll of vinyl while using a roll feeder rather than a mat. This machine cuts paper, vinyl, iron-on vinyl (or heat transfer), and bonded fabric well in addition to other materials. The machine comes with basic software that allows you to purchase and designs from their library, though you will need to upgrade to their designer software in order to use your own SVG and other type of uploaded files.

PROJECT SUPPLIES

Throughout the book we list all of the general materials and tools needed to make each project, allowing you the flexibility in many cases to choose the specific colors that you prefer. We also show you how to assemble your cut materials step by step once you have cut them out. On page 188 we offer a detailed shopping list as well as the quantity you will need for each project if you want to re-create the project exactly as we did. Instructions on cutting quantity, score lines, and additional notes are in each SVG cut file that you can reference once you open your project in the software for your machine.

PROJECT TEMPLATES

These electronic machines allow you to upload a cut file format called SVG (Scalable Vector Graphics). To download all of the design files simply go to liagriffith.com/cutting machinecrafts and access the templates featured in this book at any time by entering the code 3zRN7pAB65. (Note that these files are for personal use only and not for commercial use.)

USING SVG FILES

SVG files are created to be scalable, allowing the crafter to enlarge or reduce the design using their cutting machine software. Each machine has different steps for uploading and preparing these SVG files; and because the software can be updated, be sure to refer to the manufacturer's guide on current best steps for using these files. Often they will include videos for you to follow. At the time of publication, the Silhouette Cameo requires the Designer Software if you want to upload SVG files (so you're not limited to their templates).

SIZING YOUR SVG FILES

All of the files have been prepared at 100% for the projects in this book. You can resize to customize your cuts or design your own projects. Refer to your software manual for steps on how to enlarge or reduce a file.

CUT VS. SCORE LINES

Some of our paper projects include score lines in the designs. We have placed these on a separate layer so you can mark them in the software as a score rather than a cut. Since this step needs to be done after you upload the design into your software, remember to read and hide any design notes we have included in your file.

materials, tools, tips, and tricks

CUTTING MACHINE MATERIALS

Cutting Mats: Cricut, Sizzix. and Silhouette all offer cutting mats in 12 × 12 as well as 12 × 24 for larger cuts. The mats have a plastic sheet layer, which when removed reveals a sticky surface. This will hold your materials in place during the cut. Several brands offer different levels of stick, though for the projects in this book a standard mat will work well.

Frosted Text-weight Paper: This is one of my favorite papers to use with the cutting machine for several reasons. First, most blades will cut this paper smoothly and cleanly. Second, the frosted finish adds a gorgeous dimension to paper projects that are both flat or curled or otherwise shaped. Finally, this is my material of choice for most of my paper flowers and plants because of the illusion of added color the frosted finish gives.

Text-weight Paper: When I am unable to find a color in the frosted paper, my follow-up choice is often a colored text-weight paper for flowers, leaves, and other elements that do not require the stiffness of a card stock.

Vellum Paper: I love to add a touch of this translucent paper to lantern windows, bug wings, and even leaves. Though windows and wings look best in white vellum, you can pick colored or frosted vellum for other projects.

Glitter Paper: Some projects simply require glitter! We found that the best glitter papers for the cutting machine are those made by the cutting-machine manufacturers or papers with small glitter that does not rub off. Paper with large pieces of glitter may not cut as well and often dulls your blade.

Card Stock Paper: Many projects work best with the stiffness of card stock paper. We have found that some brands work better on the cutting machines and often mass-market brands split and peel while being removed from the mat. Make sure your blade is at the correct setting for the weight of the paper (you may want to test a scrap), and use a cutting mat with plenty of grip so your paper does not shift during the cut.

Art Paper: When I need an extra-large paper for jumbo tropical leaves or cacti plants, I find a great selection at the art supply store. Canson or comparable brands are a similar weight to card stock and will need to be trimmed to fit the 12 × 12- or 12 × 24-inch mat.

Vinyl: There are so many varieties and colors of vinyl you can purchase, and new options debut every year: matte, glossy, metallic, frosted, glitter, and brushed metal to name a few. You may have better results with your machine-branded vinyl, as it is high quality and developed to work well with the machine.

Iron-on Vinyl: Also known as heat-transfer vinyl and similar to regular vinyl, iron-on vinyl comes in many colors and finishes. Again, different brands may give you different results, so if you purchase one for the color, be sure and test a small cut with your material. We have found a few varieties that give us too much trouble so we tend to stick to the three cutting machine brands for iron-on vinyl.

note: Each project includes general materials and tools needed to make the items. For specific brands, materials, and quantities, flip to page 187.

PAPER CRAFT MATERIALS

Foam Balls and Wreaths: I prefer smooth-surface foam for wreaths and topiaries as it is sturdier than Styrofoam. I will often disguise the foam by covering it with ribbon or crepe paper before adding cut paper leaves and flowers.

Floral Wire: I prefer an 18-gauge paper-covered floral wire for crafting sturdy flower stems with a clean finish. Note that if you are making paper flowers to mix into a vase of fresh greens or flowers, choose the wire version without the paper covering so your paper blooms stay dry.

Grapevine Wreaths: I love the look of grapevine for my fall-themed designs. Find these premade wreaths at your local craft store. They make a great base for an easy-to-assemble decoration.

Brown Paper-Covered Wire: Use this wire to shape mini wreath forms; it looks pretty peeking through your paper cut shapes.

Gold Metal Hoops: You can find these hoops at fabric stores or online. They make a pretty base for small wreaths.

Wood Embroidery Hoops: The inner hoop of an embroidery frame is the right size for a mobile and can also be used as a simple wreath form.

Yarn: We use yarn for our unicorn tail and mane (page 79) as well as the carrot tops and bunny tails for the Easter brunch (page 119). You can also use yarn in place of twine or ribbon.

Twine and Thread: Cotton and baker's twine are our picks for attaching garlands, banners, and paper leis. We use gold embroidery thread when we need a metallic look for ornaments and holiday garlands. Cotton rope makes a sturdy stem for the jumbo flower backdrop (page 128) and a flexible base for the fall leaf garland (page 70).

Ribbons: Pretty ribbons add the final touches to a glitter flower wand (page 92) or mini wreaths. I also keep a stash on hand to wrap gifts or tie around the lids of festive jars .

Wood Toothpicks, Skewers, Dowels, and Beads: For my cupcake toppers, wood toothpicks or skewers are an easy way to place the paper decorations into the frosting (page 128). Throughout the book we use a variety of skewers and dowels. Check the cooking section of your local kitchen supply store for a variety of bamboo skewers and the craft store for different thicknesses and lengths of wood dowels and sizes of wood beads. You can find the long thick dowels for creating flower backdrops (page 128) at your local hardware store.

PanPastel Pigments: These pretty pastels have become a studio favorite, especially for adding a soft ombré effect to paper flower petals and leaves (page 22). You can find them online or at your local art supply store.

Markers or Colored Pencils: Water- or alcohol-based markers or colored pencils add detail to some of the paper craft projects in this book (page 78). Find a wide selection of colors at your local art supply store.

PAPER CRAFT ADHESIVES

Low-temp Hot Glue Gun: I have concluded that when using hot glue with paper, a low-temp model not only gives me the sticking power that I need but keeps blisters off the tips of my fingers. I highly recommend you trade in your high-temp glue gun for this friendlier version.

Foam Adhesive Squares: Loved by scrapbookers and card makers, these little foam risers give paper cut artwork the space between the layers to add dimension.

Glue Dots: When your project needs just a touch of stick, these dots are a great solution.

Double-sided Adhesive Roller: We keep this tape stocked in our studio for paper projects that need a smooth, thin adhesive. We recommend that you choose the permanent stick for best results.

PAPER CRAFT TOOLS

Curling Tool: Though you can use the edge of your scissors or a burnishing tool, the curling tool was designed specifically for paper curling and has a scoring tip as well.

Needle-nose Pliers and Wire Cutters: I love this two-in-one tool for my paper flowers or any project that uses wire.

Large Needle: This is a handy tool to keep in your craft toolbox when you are working with yarn and twine. You can find these jumbo needles online or at your local craft, yarn, or fabric stores.

IRON-ON VINYL TOOLS

Weeding Tool: Though this tool looks like you picked it up from your dentist's office, it is a must for easily removing the cut bits from inside the details of your design.

Iron and Ironing Surface: A standard iron and ironing board will work for iron-on vinyl. Cricut offers an iron called the Easy Press, which has become a favorite in our studio with its large surface, even temperature, and built-in timer. You can purchase a table-top ironing pad (or look up instructions online to create one) for a larger ironing surface than what your ironing board provides.

Ironing Cloth: When making projects with iron-on vinyl, I always keep an ironing cloth close by. Some plastic top layers work well with the iron directly heating the surface, while other brands do not. In that case, cover the plastic with the ironing cloth. You can make an ironing cloth from a recycled 100 percent cotton sheet or piece of white quilting fabric made from cotton.

VINYL TOOLS

Vinyl Transfer Material: This material is important for successfully transferring vinyl onto various smooth surfaces (like glass and plastic) so we keep several rolls on hand in our studio.

Burnishing Tool: I prefer the plastic burnishing tool, though you can use the edge of other flat tools.

Weeding Tool: I mentioned this tool in an earlier paragraph, but it is an important tool for your craft room because it simplifies the removal of tiny bits inside your detailed design.

SCISSORS
Every maker needs a good pair of crafting scissors. We love the full-sized 8" and the smaller 5" crafting scissor styles.

TIPS AND TRICKS

Cutting iron-on vinyl: I have made this mistake enough times that I want to loudly remind you to mirror your design before cutting iron-on vinyl. Sometimes the design will look fine in either direction but when letters or words are involved readability is key!

Removing plastic layer from iron-on vinyl: Once you peel the excess vinyl away from the design you are left with a sticky plastic. This is perfect to position your iron-on cut onto your fabric. Once you have heated the material enough to peel back the plastic layer, peel it back gently at a sharp angle. If you see spots that have not infused with the fabric, simply replace the plastic layer and reheat.

Infusing iron-on material: After pressing the heated iron to secure the design onto the fabric and peeling the plastic layer from the design, I like to cover the iron-on design with the smooth cotton cloth and give it one last press. This secures the design onto into the fabric and ensures it will last through multiple laundry cycles.

Washing iron-on vinyl: For best results, wash iron-on t-shirts and other materials on the gentle cycle in cold water, then air dry. If you need to iron out wrinkles, cover the vinyl area with a smooth cotton ironing cloth to prevent the iron-on from melting.

Removing backing paper from vinyl: I have the best results removing the backing paper when I gently peel it at a sharp angle to the vinyl design.

Washing vinyl: Though vinyl is not a permanent material, we have had very good luck with washing smooth ceramic or glass dishes that have standard vinyl designs. Some of our pieces are several years old and have been washed in the dishwasher weekly, though we do recommend you wash your pieces by hand. To permanently remove the vinyl, simply add oil to the surface to loosen the glue.

Resetting blade depth: Remember to reset your blade depth before cutting a new project. I have destroyed a few mats by cutting through them and I've also tossed some materials that did not get cut deeply enough, only to realize I missed this important step.

Keeping mats clean: The best way to keep your mats clean after use is to cover them with their plastic cover before storing. We have not found a good method to revive the stickiness of the mat, so keeping them covered between uses is our best solution to ensure the most use.

Rolling mat to remove material: An easy trick to remove almost any cut materials from your mat, especially when it is new and at the peak of its stick, is to roll the mat rather than peel off the material. If you have cut paper, this will keep your paper from curling, as it will easily pop off the sticky mat.

Using battery-operated candles: Remember to keep flames away from your paper projects. Use battery-operated candles to keep the paper flame free.

for THE HOME

Tropical Leaves

One of my favorite decorating tips for creating an inviting home is to bring the outdoors inside, and this year I'm all about tropical leaves. Create a timeless summer look that'll last all season (and longer) by making these gorgeous sculptural leaves from a heavy Canson paper. Then dab on some color and texture with PanPastel Pigments, a favorite in our studio for many different projects.

To continue the look, use the same cut files for iron-on vinyl and decorate outdoor pillows or for regular vinyl and adorn a tray that carries drinks to the backyard. These tropical leaf shapes can be used in so many different ways, just let your creativity take over!

MATERIALS & TOOLS

PAPER
- Canson paper or card stock paper
- PanPastel Pigments in shades of green
- pastel sponges
- paper curling tool
- 18-gauge green floral wire
- low-temp hot glue gun
- 12 × 24-inch cutting mat (for larger leaves)

VINYL
- cutting-machine vinyl
- vinyl transfer material
- scissors
- weeding tool
- burnishing tool

IRON-ON VINYL
- cutting-machine iron-on vinyl
- scissors
- weeding tool
- iron and ironing surface
- smooth cotton ironing cloth

PAPER STEPS

1. Cut leaves on card stock or Canson paper. For larger leaves, use 12 × 14-inch paper and large cutting mat.

2. Choose PanPastel Pigments in three shades of green. With a sponge, paint the lightest green along the score lines on the spine of the leaf.

3. Paint the midtone green in a stripe form on your leaf.

4. Begin to blend the pastels across the leaf.

5. Add the darkest pastel on edges of leaf.

6. Blend towards the center.

7. Fold leaf on scoreline in the center.

8. With curling tool, gently shape leaf.

tip: For larger leaves, use hot glue to attach 18-gauge green floral wire on the back. You can leave the wire longer to arrange the leaves in tall vases or bouquets.

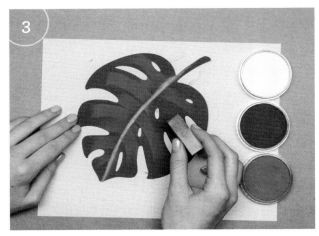

VINYL AND IRON—ON TIPS

- For multiple leaves, use sticky surface of iron-on vinyl to secure your shapes onto your fabric before you iron.

- Do not overlap your cut design onto the clear plastic of another design, as the plastic layer will prevent it from infusing with your fabric.

- Once you have initially infused the vinyl with your fabric and removed the plastic layer, cover the design with a smooth cotton cloth and give it a final press with the iron on the hottest setting to insure it has completely attached.

- When placing several layers of vinyl onto your surface you can overlap the vinyl shapes. Vinyl will stick to vinyl. Note that you will see the slight ridge of the overlap.

Scandinavian Botanicals

Based in simplicity and minimalism, these *hygge*-inspired botanical shapes lend a touch of coziness to the kitchen counter. Mixed metallic vinyl transforms a simple functional food storage container into a decorative object. Iron the leaf and flower motifs onto kitchen linens or an apron to give to your favorite chef.

MATERIALS & TOOLS

IRON-ON VINYL
- iron-on vinyl
- scissors
- weeding tool
- iron and ironing surface
- smooth cotton ironing cloth

VINYL
- cutting-machine vinyl
- vinyl transfer material
- scissors
- weeding tool
- burnishing tool

IRON-ON VINYL STEPS

1. Cut iron-on and remove the excess.

2. With weeding tool, remove detailed cuts from inside design. Examine your design carefully to ensure that all cut-outs have been removed.

3. Place design onto your fabric with the shiny plastic facing up.

4. Iron with no steam to infuse design with apron. Use cotton ironing cloth, if needed. Let cool completely, then peel back plastic layer at a sharp angle.

5. Cover design with ironing cloth and secure design onto fabric.

6. Continue process with remaining iron-on vinyl designs.

tip: Do not use steam with your iron-on material. If your material is not a natural fiber, such as cotton, linen, or silk, test a small area before transferring iron-on vinyl.

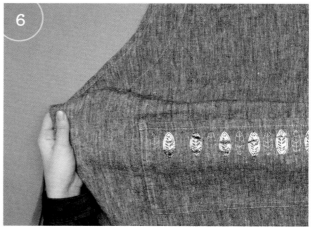

VINYL STEPS

1. Cut vinyl and remove the excess, weeding around the details from your design.

2. Cut transfer material to fit design.

3. Place transfer material over design and press with burnishing tool.

4. Peel off backing paper.

5. Place to align with second set and burnish to secure details.

6. Remove backing paper from vinyl.

7. Place vinyl onto clean surface and burnish to secure.

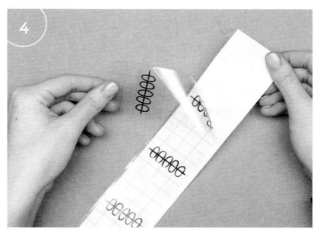

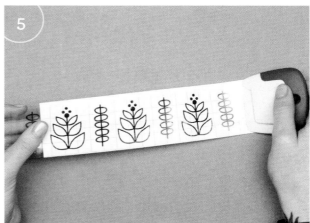

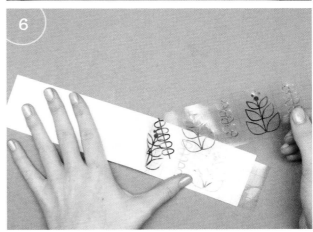

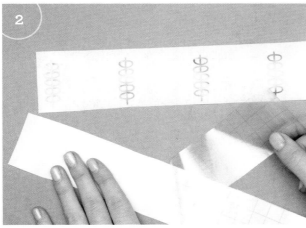

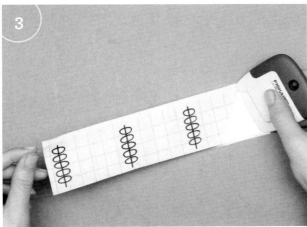

Southwest Cacti

Cactus plants seem to be *the* design accessory these days, but what if your home doesn't get full sunlight? Make your own jumbo paper cacti to bring home a bit of Southwest style. These three-dimensional sculptures can be placed into simple terra-cotta pots, painted to match your own decor. Bonus: no messy dirt to deal with!

Here, too, are four simple designs that we cut with vinyl to customize smooth stone coasters. Add your own creative touch by finding different ways to use these cute cacti templates.

MATERIALS & TOOLS

PAPER
• Canson paper or large
  card stock paper
• poster board
• low-temp hot glue gun
• paper curling tool
• spray mount or glue
• 12 × 24-inch cutting mat
• painted pot

VINYL
• cutting-machine vinyl
• vinyl transfer material
• scissors
• weeding tool
• burnishing tool
• coasters

PAPER STEPS

1. Cut pieces from card stock and one piece of base from poster board.

2. Fold large pieces of cacti along score lines.

3. With curling tool, gently shape two layers of petals of cacti flower.

4. With low-temp hot glue gun, place dot on back of one petal layer and secure it onto center of second petal layer with both sets curling upwards.

5. Use spray mount or glue to attach poster board and card stock base.

6. Slide tabs of large cacti piece into slits on top of base, leaving two base slits in between.

7. Repeat with second matching piece.

8. Slide next piece with slit at bottom over other two.

9. Press tab into base on right side.

10. Repeat with final tab to form body of cactus.

11. Add hot glue to final small top-slit piece.

12. Attach small top-slit piece to top of cactus.

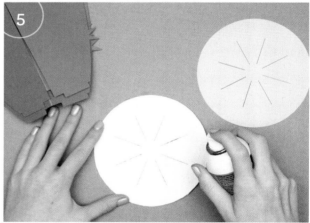

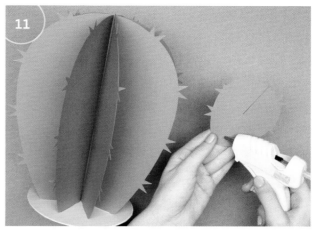

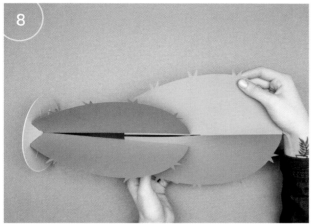

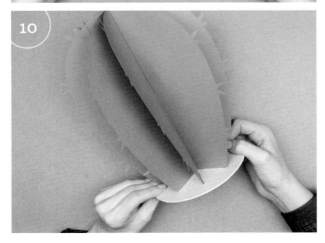

(continued)

13. Slide other pieces into slit and glue in place.

14. Glue flower to top of cactus.

15. Place into painted pot

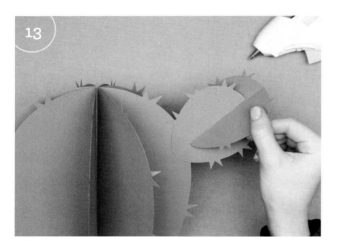

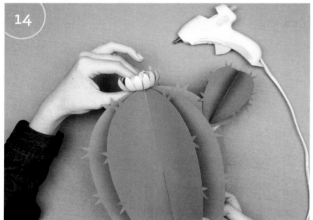

VINYL STEPS

1. Cut vinyl and remove the excess, weeding around the details from your design.

2. Cut transfer material large enough for pot and plant. Place transfer material over face of vinyl pot and press.

3. Gently peel backing paper off vinyl.

4. Place pot and transfer material over cacti and press into place.

5. Remove backing paper from vinyl.

6. Place vinyl onto clean coaster and burnish to secure.

7. Finish by adding small flower detail.

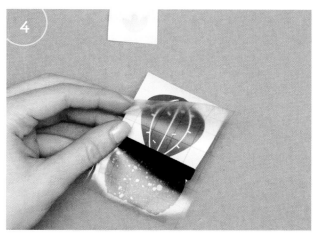

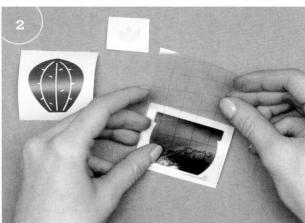

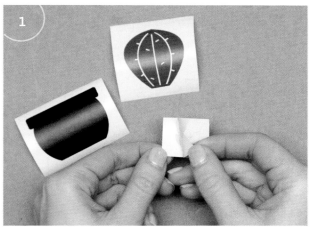

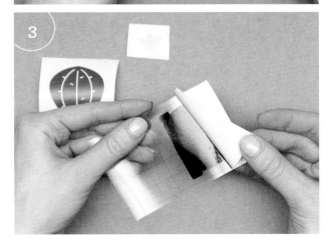

Mushroom Meadow

Another fun retro revival, mushrooms are a motif that might remind us of our grandmother's vintage kitchen. We created this mushroom meadow image to make a lovely layered piece of art that fits perfectly in a square shadow box frame. Our artwork is made from a mix of frosted text-weight and card stock papers, picked to create a soft color palette and enhance a modern or rustic setting.

The individual elements of this art make fun vinyl details for your favorite mugs. Join me for morning coffee in the garden!

MATERIALS & TOOLS

PAPER
- 6 colors of text-weight or card stock papers, each sheet 8.5 × 11 inches or larger
- 12 × 12-inch card stock paper for round window mat
- double-sided adhesive roller
- foam adhesive squares
- square frame

VINYL
- cutting-machine vinyl
- vinyl transfer material (optional)
- scissors
- weeding tool
- burnishing tool (optional)
- mugs

PAPER STEPS

1. Cut all pieces of mushroom artwork in text-weight or card stock paper.

2. Using double-sided adhesive, tape lower part of grass piece.

3. Place grass piece horizontally centered and flush with bottom of large square background paper.

4. Attach foam adhesive squares on back of fern and mushroom piece to add dimension.

5. Place fern and mushroom piece on artwork, centered horizontally.

6. Add double-sided tape to back of mushroom layer.

7. Align and place over fern and mushroom layer.

8. With double-sided tape, add mushroom tops and snail details to artwork.

9. Repeat to attach snail shell and ladybug layers.

10. Use double-sided tape on back of circular mat piece.

11. Align and place mat over layered art, adjusting grass and ferns to protrude as desired.

12. Position and secure artwork into square frame.

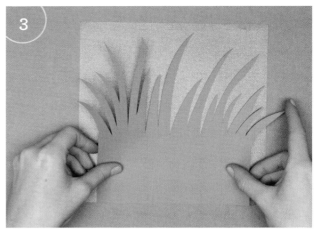

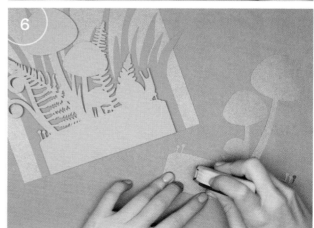

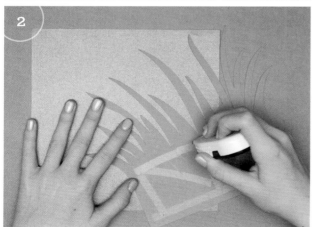

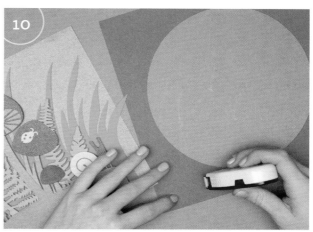

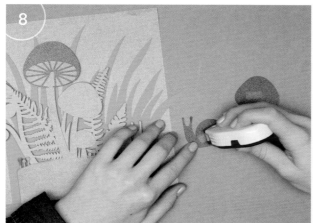

VINYL STEPS

1. Cut designs from vinyl, and peel away excess vinyl.

2. Use weeding tool to remove small pieces inside your design.

3. With point of weeding tool, remove small piece from backing paper and place onto clean, smooth surface of your mug.

4. Add second piece and press firmly onto surface.

5. Add overlay piece and press firmly to attach.

6. Transfer remaining designs onto your dishes.

tip: When applying small layered pieces of vinyl, you can place them without vinyl tranfer material. Make sure you have washed any oils or lotions off your fingers before touching the back of the vinyl and press into place with your fingers.

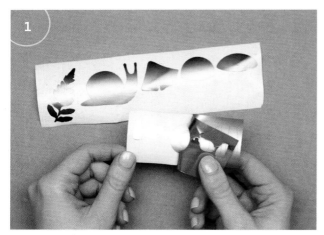

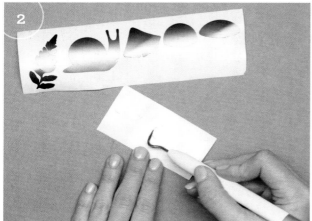

Boxwood Greenery

This evergreen boxwood wreath is one of my favorite cutting-machine projects because it is versatile. This pattern can be used for seasonal and year-round projects—wreaths, garlands, topiaries, and decorations for weddings. I sized down the cut file to make elegant mini topiaries that offer a hint of green to small spaces, kitchen counters, or bookshelves. If you want to display them outdoors, remember to protect them from water and too much sun to keep them looking fresh for years.

MATERIALS & TOOLS

- frosted text-weight paper in three shades of green
- low-temp hot glue gun
- 6-inch foam balls or foam wreath
- green crepe paper
- 12-inch wood dowels (for topiaries)

BOXWOOD GREENERY STEPS

1. Cut boxwood leaves from two or three colors of frosted paper.

2. Fold each leaf along score lines.

3. Fold leaf stems towards each other to show flat stem on back.

4. Folding all of the leaves first makes the process faster.

5. Cut a piece of green crepe paper large enough to wrap around the 6-inch foam ball or wreath. Stretch center of crepe.

6. Wrap crepe around foam ball or wreath.

7. Using low-temp hot glue gun, lightly glue crepe into place onto ball or wreath. For ball, twist ends to secure until the glue has set.

8. Clip ends of crepe.

9. Glue edges of crepe into place. Press wood dowel into place for the topiary.

10. With low-temp hot glue gun, add a line of glue down back of first boxwood stem and, starting at top, place onto ball or wreath.

11. Repeat, mixing both colors and rotating ball or wreath.

12. Continue gluing leaves to cover ball or wreath.

13. Use fingers to move leaves to cover stems.

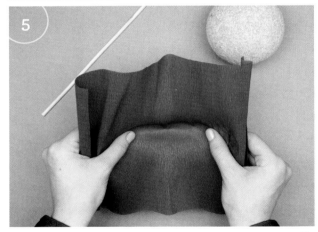

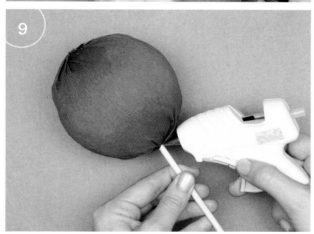

Gerbera Daisies

Not only are gerbera daisies the happiest looking flower, they are also a joy to make! These pretty blooms come together with layers of frosted paper that add softness and dimension. These gerbera daisies are delightful arranged en masse in a bouquet, as a single stem in a vase, or on top of a wrapped package for a personal touch.

MATERIALS & TOOLS

- text-weight frosted papers in petal and leaf colors
- 18-gauge green floral wire
- paper curling tool
- needle-nose pliers and wire cutters
- low-temp hot glue gun

GERBERA DAISY STEPS

1. Cut all pieces from frosted text-weight papers.

2. With curling tool, press center of each large petal to shape.

3. With curling tool, shape small and midsize flower pieces.

4. Fold leaves on score lines then shape by curling edges.

5. Using pliers, form a flat spiral at tip of floral wire.

6. With tip of wire, poke hole and slide through the center of large flower piece. Glue spiral into place.

7. Glue second large flower piece onto first with a slight rotation of petals.

8. Adhere third large flower piece, slightly rotating again.

9. Glue and layer 4 midsize flower pieces into center, rotating each layer.

10. Repeat with 4 small flower pieces, finishing with contrasting center.

11. Form cone with green sun-shaped piece and glue into place.

12. Slide cone onto wire stem, gluing into place on back of daisy.

13. Glue wire onto pale green leaf, adding second leaf on top of wire.

14. Place bloom and leaves into arrangement.

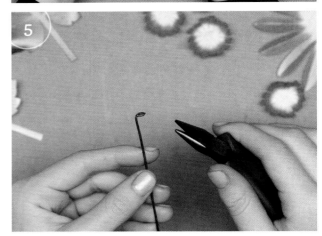

Meadow Cloche

Another way to bring the outdoors into your living space is with a scenic sculpture of a meadow contained inside a glass dome. These whimsical delights are simple to make with text-weight or card stock papers, and though we chose a soft, muted color palette for our design, you can personalize your pieces with colored papers of your choice.

MATERIALS & TOOLS

- 4 shades of text-weight or card stock papers
- double-sided adhesive roller or low-temp hot glue gun
- paper curling tool
- glass cloche

MEADOW CLOCHE STEPS

1. Cut four layers from text-weight or card stock papers.

2. Use curling tool or edge of table to curl grass layer into tube.

3. Attach edges with double-sided tape or hot glue.

4. Curl grass blades outwards with curling tool.

5. Fold leaves along score lines.

6. Shape base of darker flower with curling tool to form tube.

7. Tape or glue two edges of darker flower layer.

8. Shape and glue mouse layer and lighter flower layer. Assemble grass layer, darker flower layer, then mouse layer, sliding one inside the next.

9. Slide lighter flower layer into place.

10. Place artwork onto center of dome stand and cover with glass dome.

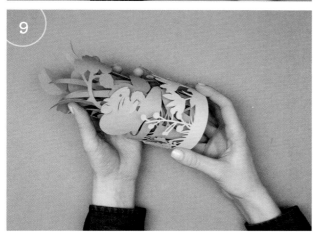

Anemone Blooms

The anemone was one of the first paper flowers I designed. I cut my original entirely with scissors. Though it was a lovely flower, the cutting machine has allowed me to add more delicate details to this bloom. A frosted text-weight paper gives me the delicate look that I love and allows the petals to easily form a cup-like shape.

Found in many shades of pink, purple, red, and classic white with a distinct black center, anemones have become a florist favorite for weddings and arrangements. I love the look of single stems lined up in a variety of vases, a bloom used as a napkin ring, or simply one flower on top of a pretty wrapped gift.

MATERIALS & TOOLS

- text-weight frosted papers in petal and leaf colors
- 18-gauge green floral wire
- paper curling tool
- needle-nose pliers and wire cutters
- low-temp hot glue gun

ANEMONE BLOOM STEPS

1. Cut all pieces from text-weight frosted paper.

2. With curling tool, shape two black center pieces.

3. Form smaller black center piece into a ball with fingers.

4. Glue ball into center of larger black stamen piece.

5. With curling tool, shape top of petals in three directions.

6. Run line of low-temp hot glue on center strip of petal base. Cross over two side strips onto the glued center to form cup.

7. Glue first three petals into triangle shape then add final three petals behind, placing each between two upper petals.

8. Add glue to back of black center piece and place into base of petals.

9. With needle-nose pliers, bend tip of 18-gauge wire at an angle.

10. Slide bent tip through hole in small back piece and cover with hot glue.

11. Place glue-covered suface onto back of flower, holding in place until glue cools.

12. Using curling tool, shape leaf in different directions.

13. Glue onto back of flower.

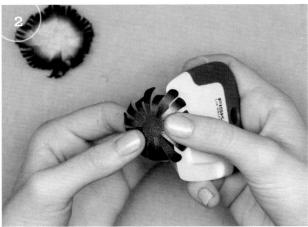

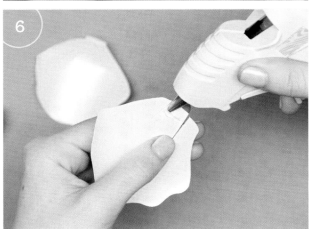

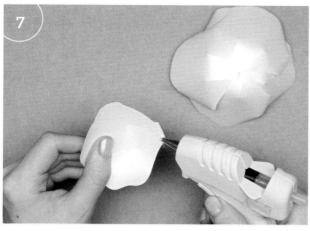

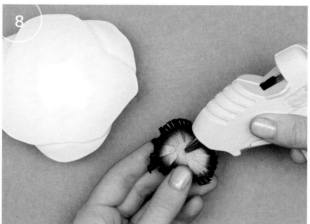

Paper Lanterns

One of our studio favorites to design for all year round, especially for the holidays, are paper lanterns. This classic garden lantern will light up your living room or the centerpiece of an outdoor party. We made our paper lanterns from a frosted text-weight paper with translucent vellum for the lantern windows.

Store your lanterns loosely in a sturdy box and you can use them again and again. Remember that any paper lantern requires battery-operated candles; keep them away from flames.

MATERIALS & TOOLS

- text-weight or card stock paper
- translucent vellum paper
- double-sided adhesive roller or low-temp hot glue gun
- mini grommets
- battery-operated candles

PAPER LANTERN STEPS

1. Cut text-weight paper or card stock for lantern and vellum rectangles for windows.

2. Apply double-sided adhesive to all four edges of each vellum piece, then place paper windows onto back side of lantern piece.

3. Fold lantern along score lines.

4. Use double-sided adhesive to connect longest edge of lantern.

5. Tape four tabs around top of lantern.

6. Press together firmly to attach four corners at top.

7. Slide tiny grommet, first through handle hole, then through top of lantern, to create moving piece.

8. Repeat on other side of handle.

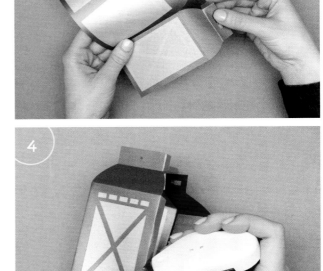

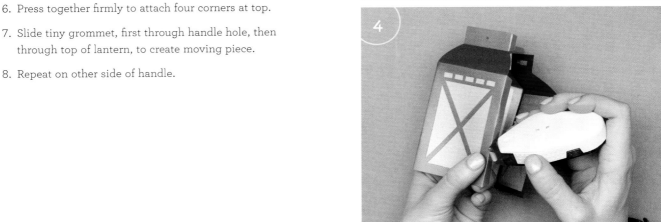

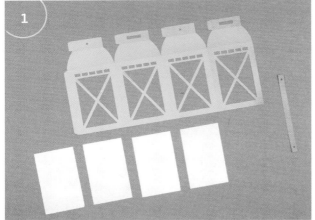

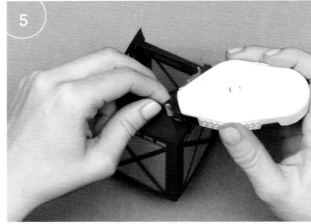

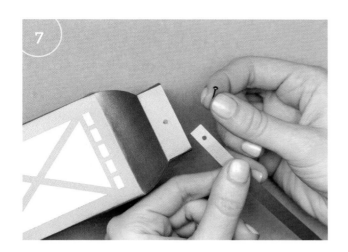

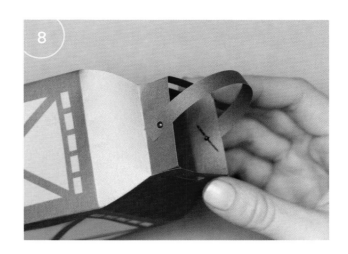

Centerpiece Succulents

Paper succulents are so versatile for decorating, as you can arrange the same set of little paper plants into many variations. Use these succulents to make a table arrangement that includes candles for a dramatic centerpiece. Or perch them on a bed of pebbles in a round terrarium. Succulents cluster beautifully together to create a lush modern wreath, or you can plant a mini one in a small pot to accompany a house-warming gift.

For these paper plants you can use text-weight paper or card stock—and pick the color palette that most pleases you.

MATERIALS & TOOLS

- text-weight or card stock papers
- paper curling tool
- low-temp hot glue gun
- 18-gauge green floral wire
- needle-nose pliers and wire cutters

tip: Some of your arrangements may work best if you put floral wire on the back of your plants to secure them into floral foam. Simply form a 2-inch U-shaped pin with your floral wire and glue it to the back of your plant. To keep the wire in place, glue a small piece of paper onto the wire where it is attached to the plant.

SUCCULENTS STEPS

1. Cut succulent pieces from text-weight or card stock papers.

2. For first succulent, use curling tool to sculpt each of three leaves into an S shape.

3. Glue the three leaves together, allowing space between each layer.

4. For second succulent, use curling tool to form fold.

5. Fold long leaves in half.

6. Arrange three leaves into plant and glue at base.

7. For third succulent, shape both three-pointed pieces with curling tool.

8. For all twelve leaves, layer and glue sides to form cup shapes.

9. Glue three cup shapes of each size to form a triangle shape.

10. Repeat process with other sizes to create four triangles.

11. Layer and glue two center pieces.

12. Glue center into smallest triangle. Continue layering triangles from smallest to largest, rotating leaves with each layer.

13. For fourth succulent, glue strip onto wire in a downwards spiral.

14. Use curling tool to shape leaves outwards.

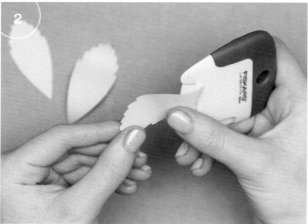

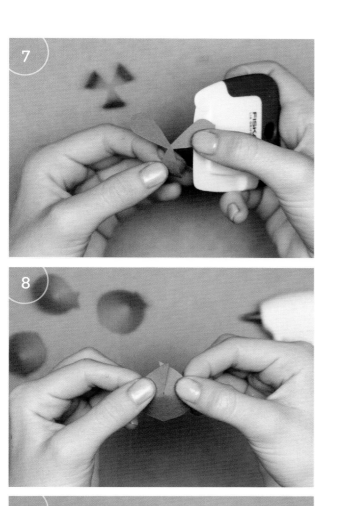

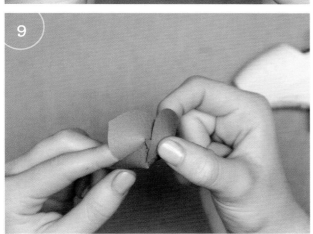

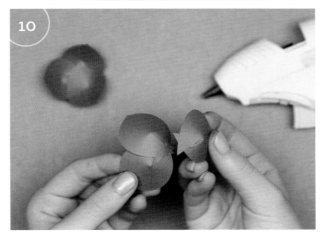

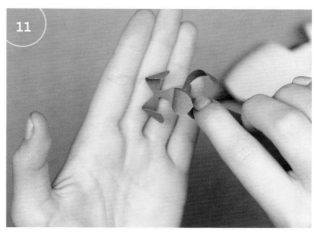

Fall Leaves

It's refreshing to celebrate the changing of seasons with new decorations. I have been making different versions of fall leaves every year and this muted color palette is my personal favorite. Add your own style by choosing a mixture of colors and textures that inspire you. Then find new ways to use the leaves throughout your home— perhaps strung together into a garland on the mantle or tucked into a napkin for a place setting.

MATERIALS & TOOLS

- frosted text-weight, vellum, or card stock papers
- paper curling tool
- low-temp hot glue gun
- grape vine wreath (for large wreath)
- 6-inch gold hoops (for mini wreaths)
- craft paint and brush (optional)

FALL LEAVES STEPS

1. Cut and score your leaves from text-weight, card stock, or vellum papers.

2. Fold leaves along score lines.

3. Use curling tool to shape leaves.

4. For leaves with multiple scores, start by folding center score line.

5. Press curling tool into score lines to shape leaf.

6. To make large wreath, glue leaves in rotation onto grapevine form.

7. For mini wreaths, glue leaves in rotation onto metal hoop.

8. For painted leaves, brush shades of paint onto paper. Let dry before shaping and folding.

tip: For our painted leaves, we cut shapes from kraft paper and added the color with paint. Gold or other metallic colors add a beautiful sheen and texture to the finished look.

tip: To make this garland, simply hot glue leaves to a length of cotton rope, overlapping the leaves so the entire strand looks even and lush.

for THE KIDS

Monster Hugs

These lovable cuties began in our studio as candy huggers, which are a sweet way to share a sentiment simply by cutting them from card stock and wrapping their little arms around a wrapped treat. Or write a note on a big paper heart and tuck the duo into a lunchbox.

Or cut them using iron-on vinyl to add a big sqeeze to tops and tees. Simply adorable!

MATERIALS & TOOLS

IRON-ON VINYL
- cutting-machine iron-on vinyl
- scissors
- weeding tool
- iron and ironing surface
- smooth cotton ironing cloth

PAPER
- card stock paper
- low-temp hot glue gun or glue dots

IRON-ON STEPS

1. Cut iron-on vinyl. Be sure to place the shiny plastic onto your mat and set your machine to cut reverse.

2. Remove the excess from around your design.

3. Use weeding tool to remove the detailed cuts in the face, horns, and feet.

4. Trim heart from sheet.

5. Place design onto your fabric, with shiny plastic facing up.

6. Iron with no steam to infuse design with shirt. Use cotton ironing cloth, if needed.

7. Peel back plastic layer at a sharp angle.

8. Cover design with cotton ironing cloth and secure design on fabric.

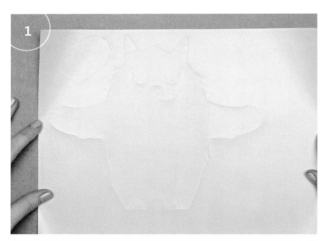

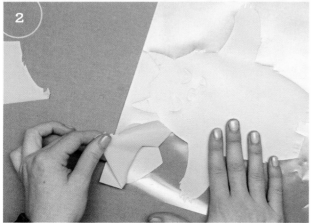

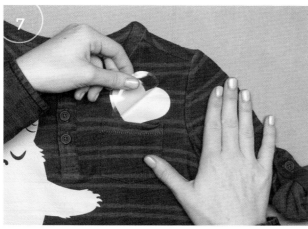

tip: For paper huggers, simply cut designs from card stock and attach your treats or notes with hot glue or glue dots. Place extra glue between treat and belly or heart layer to keep secure.

Unicorns and Rainbows

Bring some magic into your child's bedroom with a unicorn pillow that will look great on the bed. With the same materials and steps, you can simply size down the design to make a personalized t-shirt or pajama top. For the desk area, string up a unicorn garland complete with yarn tails and manes with colorful rainbows to create a stimulating homework nook.

MATERIALS & TOOLS

IRON-ON VINYL
- cutting-machine iron-on vinyl
- scissors
- weeding tool
- iron and ironing surface
- smooth cotton ironing cloth

PAPER GARLAND
- card stock paper
- glitter paper
- pink yarn for mane and tail
- pink baker's twine
- washi tape
- pink marker or colored pencil
- double-sided adhesive roller
- scissors
- small knitting needle

IRON-ON STEPS

1. Cut iron-on vinyl in reverse. Weed and remove all excess vinyl. Trim pieces to separate.

2. Place unicorn head in center of pillow fabric.

3. Using iron on high heat, cover vinyl with cotton cloth and iron to infuse material with fabric.

4. Let cool, then gently peel back plastic at a sharp angle.

5. Position unicorn mane and pink cheek.

6. Cover with cotton cloth and iron to infuse material with fabric.

7. Let cool, then gently peel back plastic at a sharp angle.

8. Repeat process with stars and unicorn horn. Once all elements are in place, cover entire unicorn head with cotton cloth and iron to secure design onto fabric.

9. Place pillow fill into cover.

10. Add a little unicorn magic to your decor!

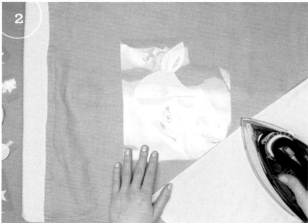

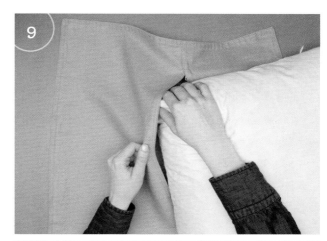

PAPER GARLAND STEPS

1. Cut unicorn layers from card stock and glitter paper.

2. Using pale pink marker, draw cheeks on the unicorn.

3. Apply double-sided adhesive to back of top unicorn layer.

4. Position and press top unicorn layer onto glitter layer.

5. Cut seven strands of pink yarn, each 8 inches long. Fold first piece in half.

6. String two ends of yarn through first hole. Pull ends through loop to secure yarn on neck.

7. Repeat with remaining holes, doubling the yarn for tail.

8. Use small knitting needle to fray yarn.

9. Trim mane and tail with small scissors.

10. Cut rainbow, cloud, and star pieces from card stock paper.

11. Apply double-sided adhesive to back of center rainbow layer.

12. Position and press center rainbow layer onto back layer.

13. Repeat with third rainbow layer and clouds.

14. Create garland by attaching unicorn and rainbow ornaments to pink baker's twine with pretty washi tape.

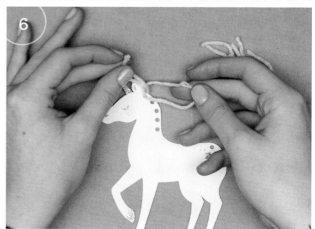

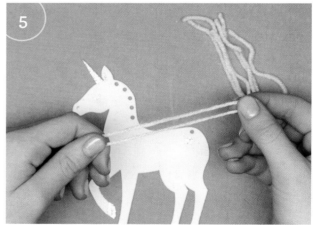

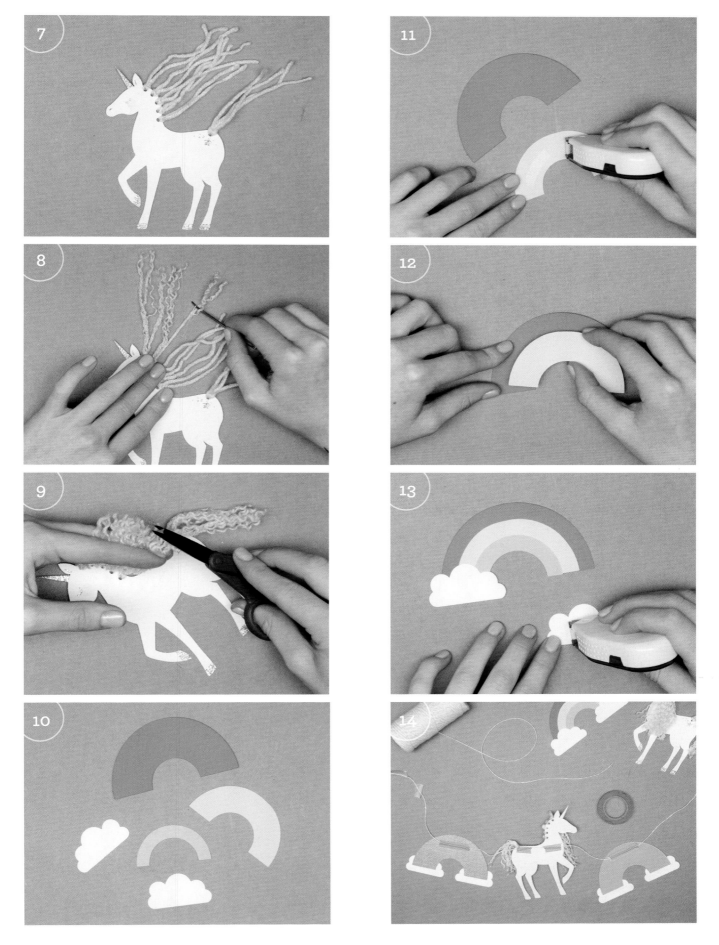

Natural History of
INSECTS

1. Caterpillar 2. Bumlebee 3. Beetle 4. Ladybug 5. Grasshopper

Friendly Insects

Arrange a set of insects into an identification chart that elevates a school project into wall art; then reward your little explorers with an honor patch to add to their explorer vests. Let your imagination run wild with different ways to use these colorful bugs with different applications and materials.

MATERIALS & TOOLS

PAPER POSTER
- text-weight or card stock papers
- white vellum
- 11 × 17-inch cream card stock
- cotton twine
- two 11-inch-long wood trim pieces
- double-sided adhesive roller
- craft tape
- low-temp hot glue gun

IRON-ON PATCH
- cutting-machine iron-on vinyl
- wool-blend felt
- fusible bonding web
- scissors
- weeding tool
- iron and ironing surface
- smooth cotton ironing cloth

PAPER POSTER STEPS

1. Cut all pieces from text-weight or card stock papers and vellum for bee wings.

2. Apply double-sided adhesive onto back of top layers of bugs and wing edges.

3. Position and press layers into place.

4. Repeat process with leaf layers.

5. Print poster design onto 11 × 17-inch cream card stock and adhere bugs into place.

6. Finish design by adding leaves.

7. Tape cotton twine to hang poster.

8. Glue 11-inch-long wood trim pieces to back and front of top of poster art.

tip: Your printable poster design is in the online folder with all of the SVG cut files in the form of a PDF. When printing, make sure to select "full size" in your print menu. If you don't have a large-format printer, you can visit your local office supply store to print the poster.

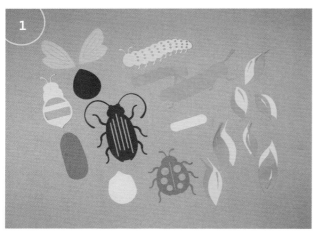

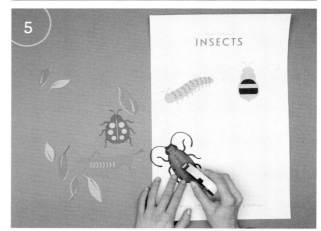

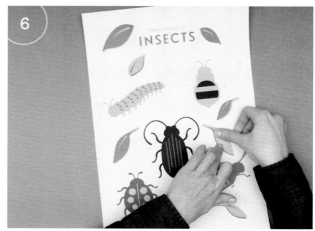

7

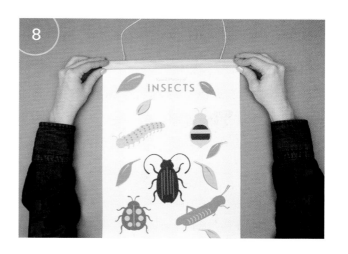

8

IRON-ON PATCH STEPS

1. Cut iron-on vinyl with patch design. Remove surrounding extra vinyl.

2. Use weeding tool to remove bug shape from center of design.

3. Iron vinyl design onto wool-blend felt square in a contrasting color.

4. Trim patch from felt.

5. Cut fusible bonding web to size of patch and iron patch onto vest. Be sure to use cotton ironing cloth to protect your vinyl from direct contact with the iron.

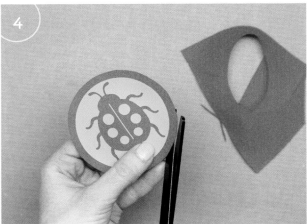

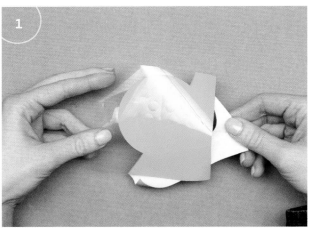

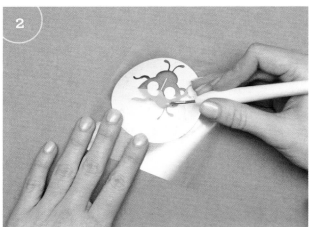

Fairy Crown and Flower Wand

Every little princess needs a crown. We made our pretty floral version with pink glitter card stock and created a flowery wand to match. These crowns are so simple to assemble that they would make coveted favors for all the little princesses at your party.

MATERIALS & TOOLS

- glitter card stock
- 12-inch wood dowel
- 1-inch and ¼-inch wide ribbon
- low-temp hot glue gun
- scissors

FAIRY CROWN AND WAND STEPS

1. Cut crown pieces from glitter card stock.

2. Place dots of hot glue to two points on back of large flower.

3. Position and attach both sides of crown with flower in center.

4. Size and glue back of crown to fit head.

5. Cut wand pieces from glitter card stock.

6. Glue flower detail pieces together so that both sides have glitter.

7. Attach 1-inch wide ribbon to base of 12-inch wood dowel.

8. Wind ribbon up dowel at a slight angle and glue into place at top.

9. Cut two pieces of ¼-inch wide ribbon, each 12 inches long.

10. Glue at half point to top of stick.

11. Glue stick and flower details to back of large flower.

12. Add generous amount of glue to large flower and position second flower to align.

13. Press into place and let cool.

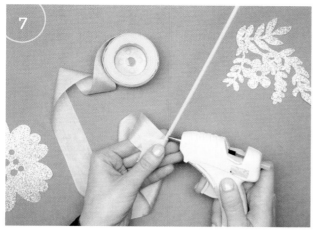

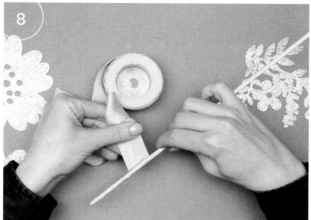

Paper Boats

So effortless to make from paper and a wood skewer, these little boats can be used as place cards for a summer dinner or favors for a child's birthday party. Create your fleet from a mix of colored card stock papers or choose wood-print paper for the boat and cut the sails from a white vellum.

I can also imagine these little paper boats as a colorful mobile in a nursery. What creative way would *you* use them?

MATERIALS & TOOLS

- card stock paper or
  wood-print paper and
  white vellum
- 7-inch wood dowel or skewer
- low-temp hot glue gun
- paper curling tool

PAPER BOAT STEPS

1. Cut boat pieces from card stock paper or wood-print paper and white vellum.

2. Fold base of boat along score line.

3. Fold four tabs along score lines.

4. Using low-temp hot glue gun, glue tabs on base of boat.

5. Glue and assemble sides of boat.

6. Fold boat seat along score lines.

7. Glue seat into center of boat.

8. Seat will help hold shape of boat and hold sails.

9. Glue small sail onto 8-inch wood dowel.

10. Shape large sail with curling tool.

11. Glue tip of top and bottom of sail onto smaller sail and wood dowel.

12. Slide dowel into hole in seat and glue to base of boat.

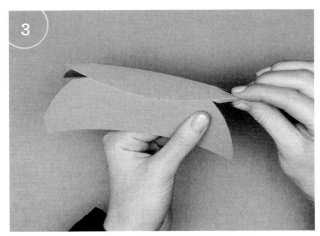

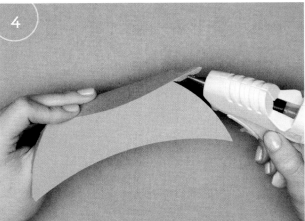

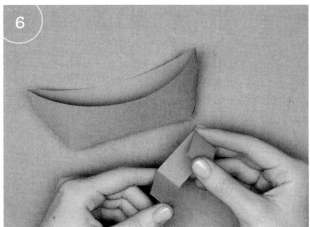

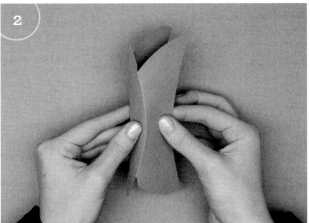

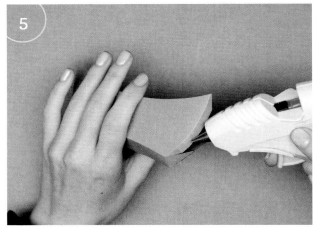

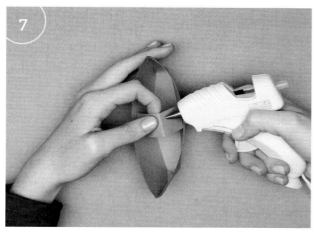

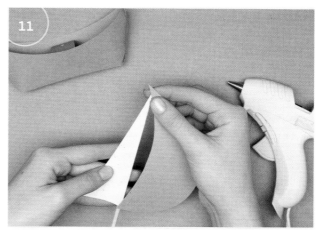

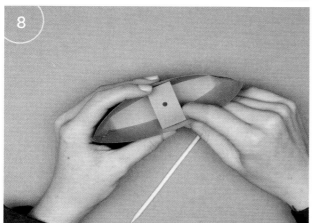

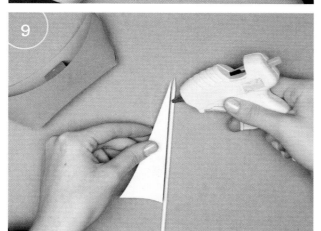

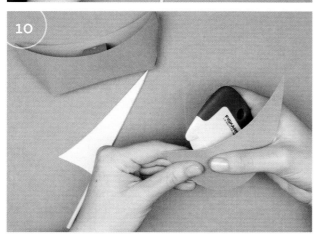

Forest Friends

It doesn't get much sweeter than a happy bear hugging a mushroom. Featuring a cute-as-can-be crew of bears, mushrooms, and leaves, this woodland-themed baby mobile is the most darling of decorations for your baby's room. Your little ones will be both comforted and charmed by this whimsical work of art.

We have also designed the bear in an iron-on version that makes a perfect gift for the little one. Use an extra paper bear to decorate the package.

MATERIALS & TOOLS

PAPER MOBILE
- text-weight or card stock paper
- needle and sewing thread
- cotton twine
- 10-inch embroidery hoop
- double-sided adhesive roller
- paper curling tool
- scissors
- large needle
- 1-inch wood bead

IRON-ON ONESIE
- cutting-machine iron-on vinyl
- weeding tool
- iron and ironing surface
- smooth cotton ironing cloth

PAPER MOBILE STEPS

1. Cut all shapes from text-weight or card stock paper.

2. Turn over the detailed bear. Apply double-sided tape to the back side, staying clear of the paws.

3. Attach detailed bear to silhouette of bear.

4. Repeat steps with mushrooms and acorns.

5. Use hot glue to attach mushroom and leaf under bear arms.

6. Fold leaves in half along score lines.

7. Use curling tool to shape leaves.

8. Use needle to create tiny hole at top of bear head. String thread through hole.

9. Add holes and string to all of the leaves, acorns, and mushrooms.

10. Remove outer piece from embroidery hoop. Tie one piece of cotton twine onto inner hoop.

11. Add two more pieces of cotton twine onto hoop. Gather all three pieces and tie.

12. Using large needle, slide wood bead onto gathered twine.

13. Tie three bears onto hoop centered between each cotton twine.

14. Finished by tying all leaves, acorns, and mushrooms onto mobile.

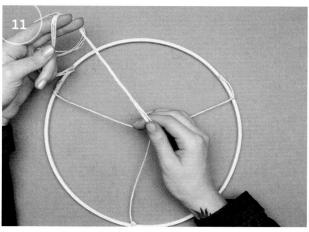

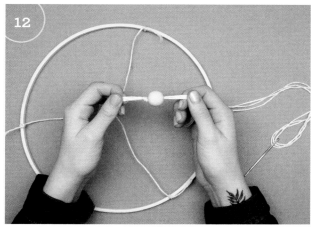

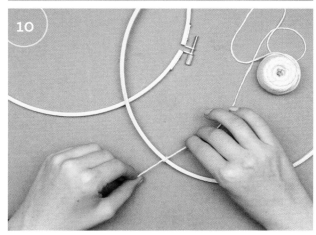

IRON-ON ONESIE STEPS

1. Cut design on back side of iron-on material. Remove excess and use weeding tool to remove details.

2. Place bear onto center of baby onesie.

3. With hot iron and no steam, infuse the design with the onesie. Use smooth cotton ironing cloth, if needed. Remove plastic layer at a sharp angle.

4. Align and place mushroom design onto bear.

5. Cover with smooth cotton ironing cloth and infuse mushroom with onesie. Remove plastic layer at a sharp angle. Once both elements are in place, cover entire motif with cotton cloth and iron to secure design onto fabric.

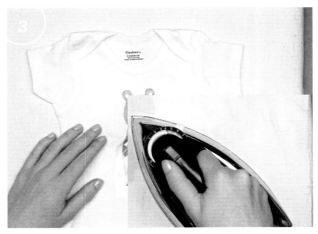

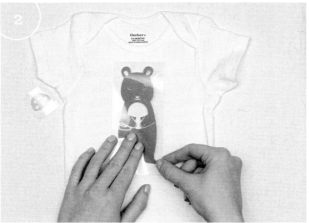

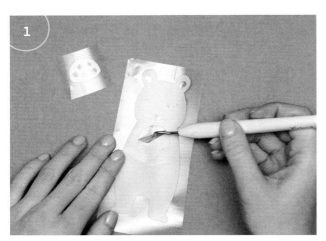

Blossom Letters

Letters can personalize anything and these templates give you the complete alphabet so you can exercise your creativity. Design a t-shirt with a pretty monogram or use vinyl cut letters to adorn bedroom walls. You could also add a letter to a mug, cut the letters out of card stock to form a banner for a party, or create a piece of art by placing a monogram in a pretty frame.

tip: For this t-shirt, we used foil iron-vinyl, and when working with foil heat transfer material, it's especially important that you let the iron-on cool before peeling off the backer plastic.

MATERIALS & TOOLS

VINYL
· cutting-machine vinyl
· vinyl transfer material
· scissors
· weeding tool
· burnishing tool

IRON-ON VINYL
· cutting-machine iron-on vinyl
· weeding tool
· iron and ironing surface
· smooth cotton ironing cloth

VINYL STEPS

1. Cut letters from vinyl, remove excess, and use weeding tool to remove details from center of design.

2. Cut tranfer material the size of the letters, place, and burnish.

3. Cut a long strip of paper the length of your letters. Tape paper onto wall, using a level to ensure it is straight.

4. Remove backing paper from letters.

5. Using paper on wall as a baseline, place vinyl onto surface.

6. Use burnishing tool to secure onto wall.

7. Peel transfer material off wall at a sharp angle.

8. Repeat with remaining letters, using burnishing tool to remove bubbles.

tip: You can reuse your transfer material several times if you keep it clean from dust and debris. One piece easily transferred all four of our letters for this project.

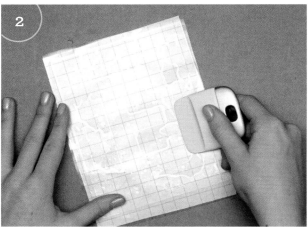

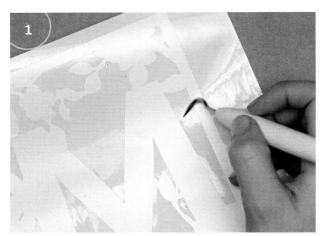

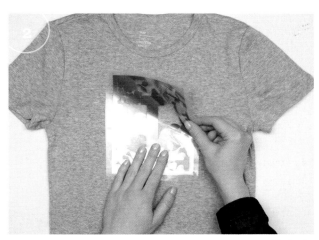

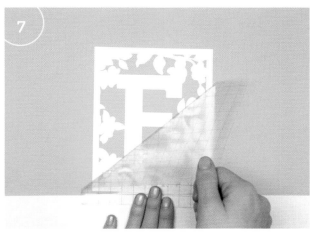

IRON-ON VINYL STEPS

1. Cut iron-on vinyl with shiny plastic side facing mat and reversing design. Remove excess vinyl and weed details.

2. Place design, plastic side up, onto t-shirt.

3. Use hot iron with no steam to infuse design with fabric. Use smooth cotton ironing cloth, if needed.

4. Let vinyl cool completely. Remove plastic layer by gently peeling at a sharp angle.

5. Cover design with cotton ironing cloth and iron to secure design onto fabric.

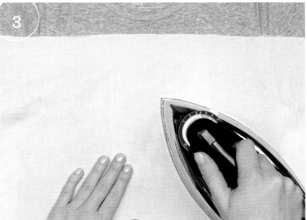

for CELEBRATIONS

Love and Hearts

With a basic straight stitch on your sewing machine, and three layers of paper cut hearts, you can make a dimensional heart garland for your table. To add to your display, cut words from paper or vinyl and place onto your wall and glass treat jars. It's a look that everyone will love!

MATERIALS & TOOLS

TREAT JAR VINYL
- cutting-machine vinyl
- vinyl transfer material
- scissors
- weeding tool
- burnishing tool
- glass jar

PAPER GARLAND
- text-weight or card stock papers in a variety of glitter, frosted, and vellum
- sewing machine and thread
- scissors
- wood toothpicks (for toppers)
- low-temp hot glue gun (for toppers)

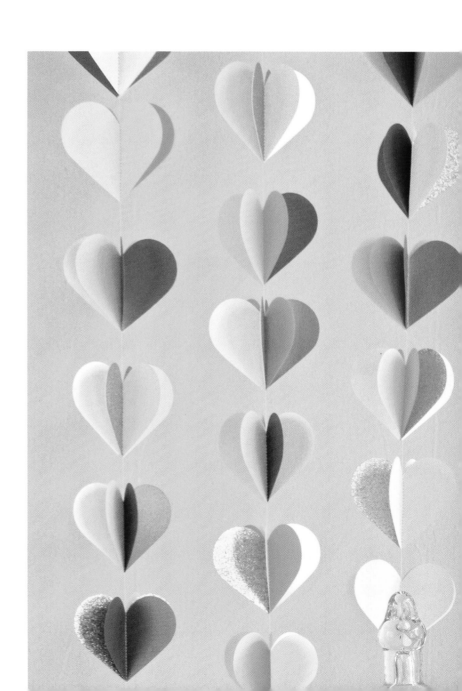

TREAT JAR VINYL STEPS

1. Cut design from vinyl. Peel away excess vinyl.

2. Use weeding tool to remove details.

3. Cut transfer material the size of the design and burnish over letters.

4. Peel away from backing paper.

5. Add vinyl hearts onto transfer material with sticky side of hearts facing up.

6. Place design onto clean glass jar, burnish, and peel back transfer material at a sharp angle.

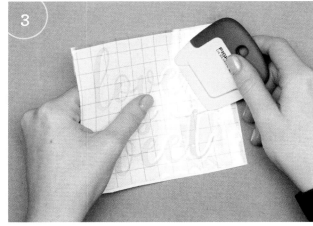

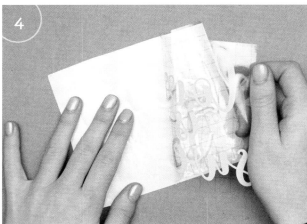

PAPER GARLAND STEPS

1. Cut sheets of hearts in a mix of papers.

2. Arrange hearts into stacks of three different colors.

3. Using sewing machine, straight stitch through center of hearts in a row.

4. For garland, keep hearts attached to each other and press layers of hearts open to form three-dimensional shapes.

5. For treat toppers, trim strand of hearts and press layers of hearts open to form three-dimensional shapes.

6. For treat toppers, apply hot glue onto toothpicks and secure onto base of hearts.

Bunnies and Carrots

Why not make your Easter brunch table as playful as possible? Set the table with polka dot paper cut placemats, and top your settings with bunny favors. We filled our basket with carrot treat boxes and added paper bunny ears to the drinking glasses. To keep your guests entertained, fill a carrot-themed cup with crayons for them to help decorate the kraft paper table cover.

MATERIALS & TOOLS

- card stock paper in orange and white
- text-weight paper in green
- white and green yarn
- small white paper cups
- small pom-pom maker
- low-temp hot glue gun
- 4-inch wood dowels
- scissors
- small milk bottles
- pink marker or colored pencil
- double-sided adhesive roller
- large needle
- paper curling tool
- 3 × 6-inch piece of cardboard

CARROT TREAT BOX STEPS

1. Cut and score carrot using card stock paper.

2. Fold carrot along score lines.

3. Apply hot glue to tab on side of carrot.

4. Hold carrot in place until glue is cool.

5. Holding 3 × 6-inch piece of cardboard vertically, wrap green yarn around it lengthwise twelve times.

6. Cut a 12-inch piece of yarn. Slide one end of the piece between the cardboard and the wrapped yarn, slide it up to top of cardboard, and tie yarn into bundle.

7. Slide yarn off of cardboard.

8. Cut another 12-inch piece of yarn. Wrap it around top of yarn bundle and tie.

9. Continue to wrap bundle several times, then thread one end of yarn through large needle and slide needle through wrap to join end with bundle of yarn. Repeat with second end.

10. Trim ends of yarn to create tassel.

11. Glue two tabs at top of carrot opening and fill your box with treats.

12. Thread your tassel strings through holes in top and tie to close.

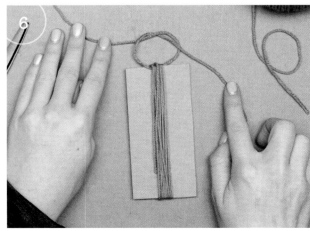

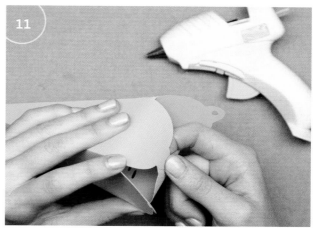

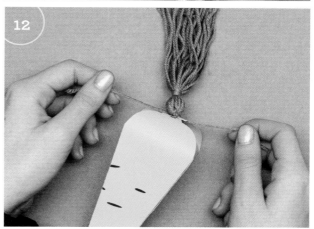

CARROT CUP STEPS

1. Cut carrot wrap from card stock paper and carrot top from text-weight paper.

2. Glue tab end of wrap onto paper cup.

3. Encircle cup with carrot wrap around and glue end to secure.

4. Use curling tool or edge of table to shape carrot top.

5. Glue wood dowel at base of carrot top.

6. Wrap paper around dowel.

7. Glue end to secure onto dowel.

8. Use fingers to spread fringed paper.

9. Shape tips of fringe with curling tool. Place crayons into cup, adding carrot top into center of bundle.

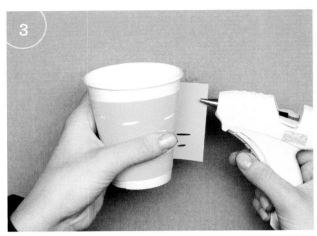

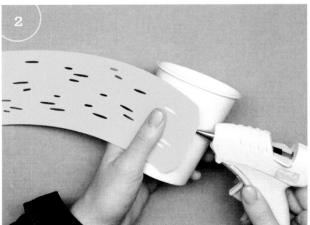

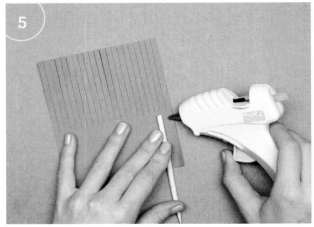

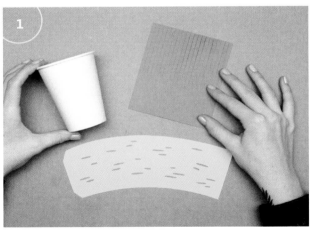

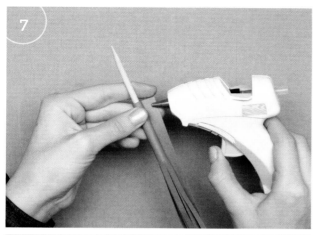

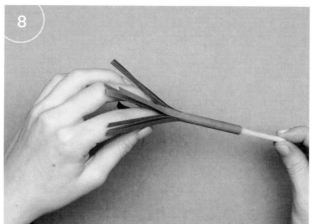

BUNNY EAR STEPS

1. Cut bunny ears from card stock paper.

2. Color in details of bunny ears with marker or colored pencil.

3. Wrap bunny ears around top of cup or milk bottle.

4. Trim to fit.

5. Use hot glue to secure into place.

6. Your bunny ear topper is ready to delight!

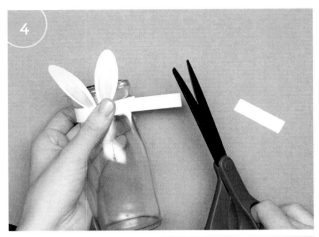

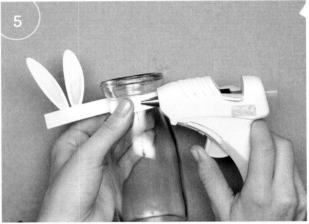

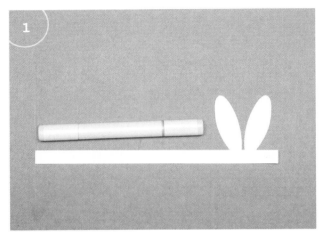

BUNNY TREAT BOX STEPS

1. Cut bunny box from card stock paper. Face details can be cut from text-weight or card stock paper.

2. Glue eyes and nose onto ear side of box.

3. Use marker or colored pencil to add cheeks.

4. With same marker or colored pencil, add detail onto ears.

5. Glue whiskers onto cheeks.

6. Turn box over and fold up four sides along score lines.

7. Use curling tool to shape all sides of box.

8. Slide bunny ears into tabs to create box.

9. With smallest pom-pom maker, form a white tail.

10. Glue tail onto back of box.

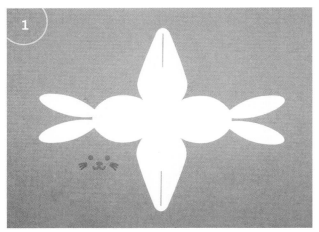

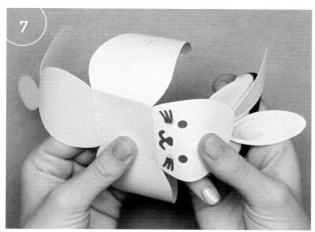

Spring Garden Party

These easy-to-make paper flowers are a sweet way to add a little spring to your party. Make a mini flower garden to decorate your cake and cupcakes with a mix of spring colors in frosted papers. Place your blooming cupcakes into their own scalloped paper flowerpots.

Using the same flower designs, transform the cuts into a jumbo flower backdrop for your cake display or a photo booth.

MATERIALS & TOOLS

- frosted text-weight papers for flowers
- card stock or wood-print paper for cupcake wraps
- small gold beads
- wood toothpicks and small skewers
- paper curling tool
- low-temp hot glue gun
- 1-inch wood beads
- gold paint or pen
- five 5-foot long pieces cotton cord or clothesline rope
- 3-foot wood dowel, 1-inch in diameter
- 2 removable coat hooks
- tape

CAKE DECOR STEPS

1. Cut flowers and leaves from frosted text-weight paper.

2. Fold leaves along score lines.

3. Shape three-pointed petals with curling tool.

4. Glue small yellow stamen to tip of toothpick.

5. Wrap yellow stamen around toothpick and glue into place.

6. Slide two layers of three-pointed petals onto toothpick and glue into place.

7. Petals will align to create six-pointed flower.

8. Fold leaf, wrap around toothpick, and glue into place.

9. Shape petal strip with curling tool.

10. Shape flower petals with curling tool.

11. Glue petal strip onto wood skewer, wrap, and glue into place with petals curling outwards.

12. Slide two layers of matching petals onto wood skewer and glue into place with petals curling outwards.

13. Fold leaf, wrap around wood skewer, and glue into place. Repeat with second leaf.

14. Glue yellow leaves to top of toothpick.

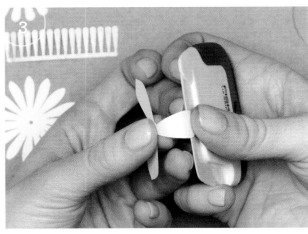

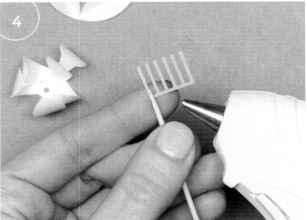

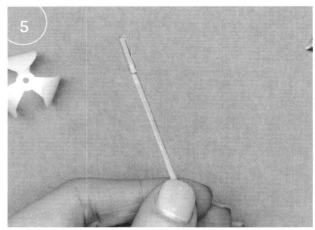

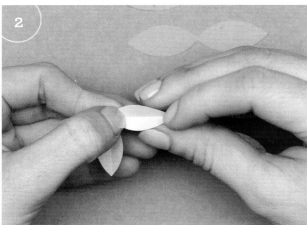

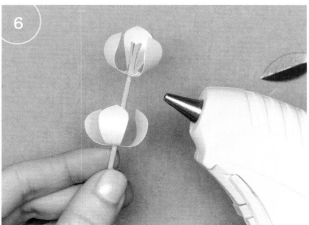

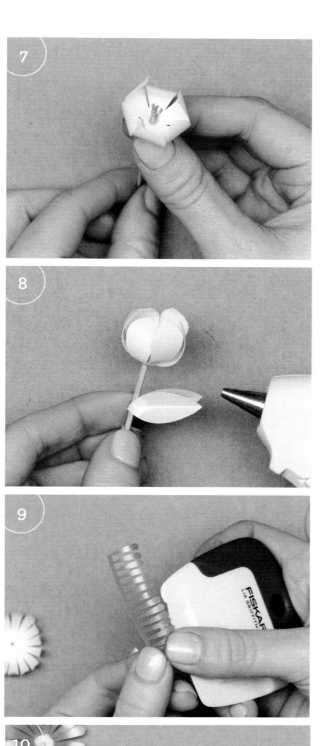

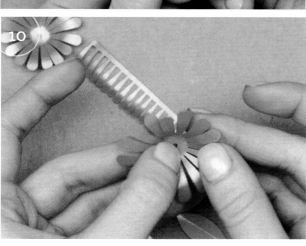

CAKE DECOR STEPS (CONTINUED)

15. Shape petals with curling tool.

16. Glue gold bead onto tip of wood skewer.

17. Slide two layers of pink petals onto skewer and glue into place.

18. Petals will be curling upwards with second layer rotating.

19. Wrap two sets of leaves around wood skewer and glue into place.

20. Repeat flower and leaf assembly for quantity needed for cake and cupcake decorations.

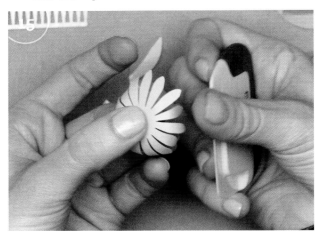

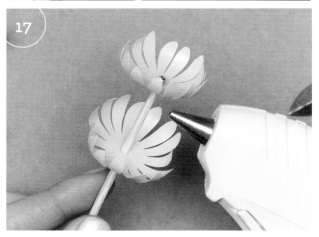

PHOTO BACKDROP STEPS

1. Cut flowers and leaves from frosted text-weight paper.

2. Use curling tool to shape petals.

3. Fold petals at base to form arch.

4. Repeat with second flower piece, then layer and glue smaller piece inside larger piece.

5. Use curling tool to shape strip of petals.

6. Roll strip with petals curling outwards and glue into position.

7. Glue rolled piece into center of flower.

8. Shape three-pointed petals with curling tool.

9. Repeat with second piece, then glue together at base to form six-pointed petals.

10. Shape yellow stamen with curling tool.

11. Roll with curl shaping outwards and glue into center of flower.

12. Fold all leaves along score lines.

13. Paint 1-inch wood beads with gold pen or paint.

14. Tie cotton clothesline ropes onto wood dowel, spacing them 5 to 6 inches apart.

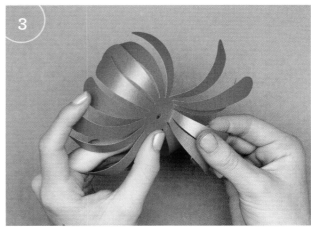

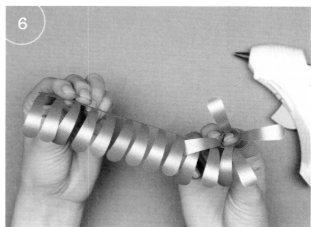

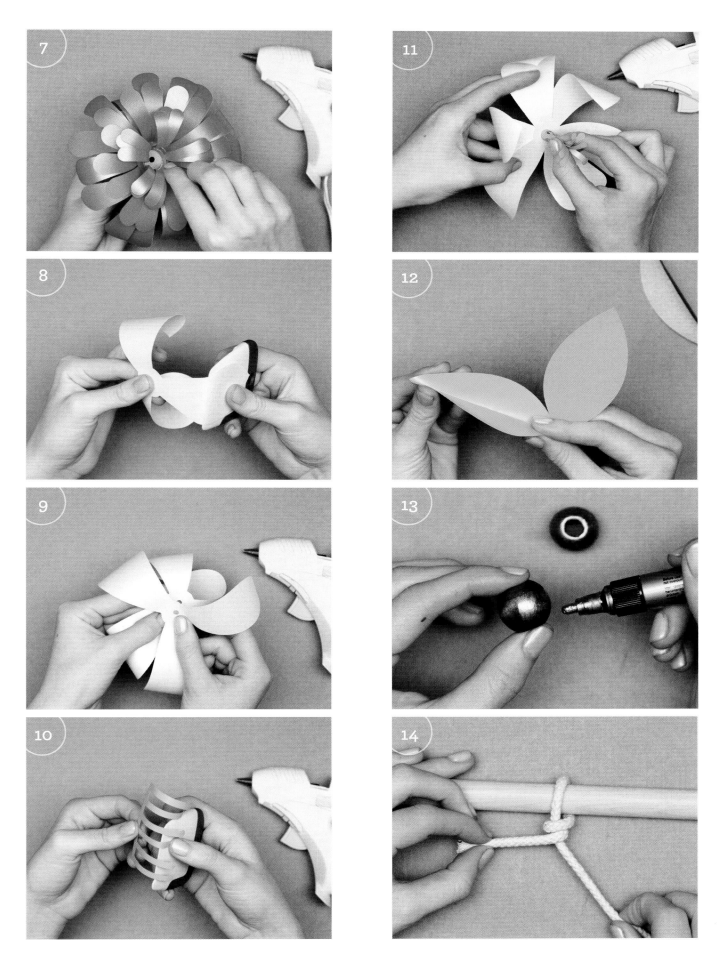

PHOTO BACKDROP STEPS (CONTINUED)

15. Glue one rope knot into place.

16. Use tape to create pointed tip at end of rope, making it easy to slide paper flowers onto rope.

17. Slide gold bead onto rope.

18. Slide pink flower onto rope under bead.

19. Glue petals onto bead and yellow leaves onto rope under bloom.

20. Slide rope through center of stamen on white flower and glue into place.

21. Wrap leaves around rope and glue into place.

22. Slide coral bloom onto rope, wrap leaves around rope, and glue the bloom and leaves into place.

23. Repeat steps 15 to 22 for other ropes on dowel, adding 3 flowers to each rope and changing flower order for variety. Install dowel on a wall using two removable coat hooks so ropes hang vertically.

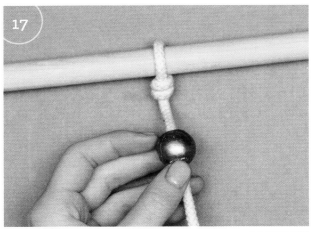

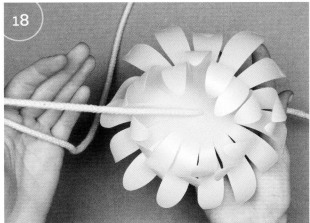

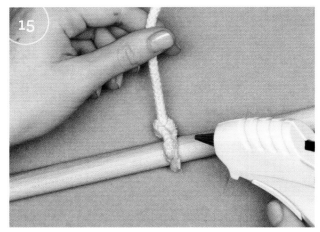

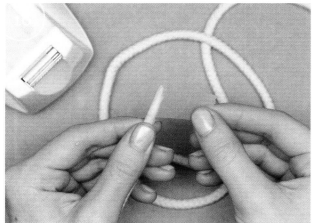

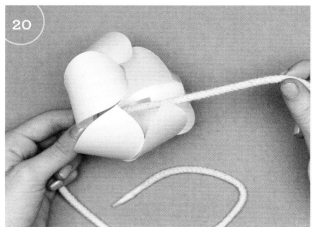

Peony Bouquet

Flowers made from frosted paper are like little sculptures; add them to a wedding bouquet for a piece of art the bride can carry on her wedding day and keep long after as a loving reminder. The text-weight sheet allows the paper to form and curl easily, creating a soft translucent look to the petals. The frosted finish catches the light, giving the illusion of multiple shades in your paper blooms.

Paper peonies can be used to decorate your wedding or event in the way of corsages, napkin rings, and centerpieces.

MATERIALS & TOOLS

- text-weight frosted paper for petals
- card stock paper for leaves
- 18-gauge green floral wire
- paper curling tool
- needle-nose pliers and wire cutters
- low-temp hot glue gun

PEONY STEPS

1. Cut petals from text-weight frosted paper and leaves from text-weight or card stock.

2. Using curling tool, shape each small and medium petal in three directions.

3. Shape large petals in several directions to form cup shape.

4. Shape tips of stamen fringe with curling tool.

5. Bend tip of 18-gauge wire with needles nose pliers.

6. Glue end of fringe to wire and wrap around with fringe curling outwards.

7. Glue end of stamen fringe into place.

8. Slide first small petals onto wire and glue at base of stamen.

9. Repeat with second small petals, rotating then gluing petals.

10. Slide third small petals onto wire, rotate, and glue into place.

11. Repeat steps with three medium petals.

12. Slide large two-petal piece onto wire and glue at base of bloom.

13. Repeat with final two pieces, rotating as you glue into place.

14. Use fingers to shape petals towards center.

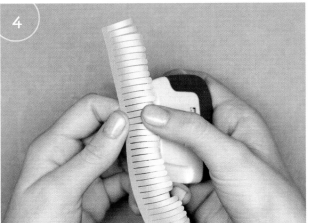

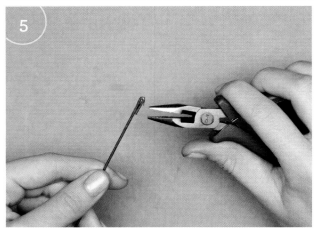

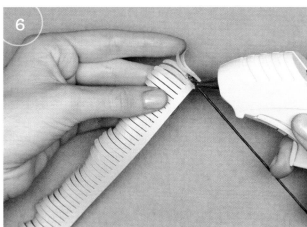

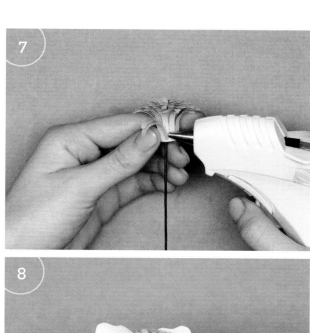

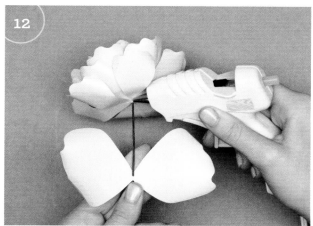

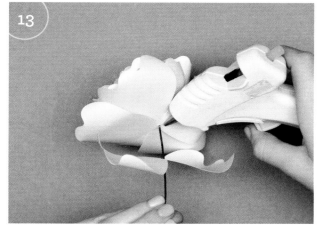

PEONY STEPS (CONTINUED)

15. Use curling tool to shape sepal.

16. Glue tab and form cone shape. Slide sepal onto wire stem and glue into place under flower.

17. Shape leaves with curling tool.

18. Glue 18-gauge wire onto leaf.

19. Add extra glue on top of wire and cover with second leaf.

tips: Mixing paper flowers with real greenery and filler flowers is a simple way to create a gorgeous look. Choose greens and filler to add texture, color, and depth to your arrangement.

If you are placing your paper blooms into a vase with live greens or flowers, remember to use floral wire that is not paper covered. This will keep your paper flowers dry so that you can use them again in another arrangement.

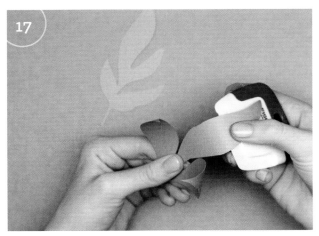

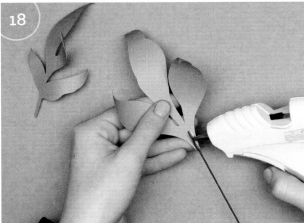

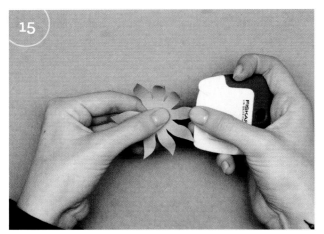

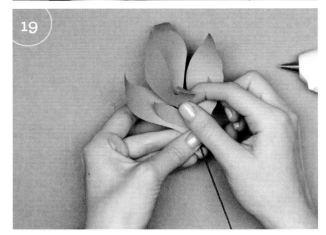

Tropical Party

Can't you just feel the ocean breeze? Imagine creating a paper lei for each of your party guests and decorating their beverage straws with a pretty paper hibiscus bloom. Don't stop there . . . decorate your table with large paper palm and monstera leaves and top things off with a flower garland and well-placed hibiscus. For dessert, decorate your tropical cupcakes with mini monstera leaves and a matching wrap. Thanks to the quick work of your cutting machine, this will be a party that everyone will talk about.

MATERIALS & TOOLS

LEIS
- text-weight frosted paper in petal and leaf colors
- green baker's twine
- paper curling tool
- large needle
- low-temp hot glue gun

CUPCAKES
- text-weight paper
- wood toothpicks
- low-temp hot glue gun

DECORATIVE LEAVES
- Canson paper, card stock paper, or text-weight frosted paper
- 12 × 24-inch cutting mat (for larger leaves)

LEI STEPS

1. Cut flowers and leaves from text-weight frosted paper.

2. Shape all petals with curling tool.

3. Glue tabs on flowers and attach to side to create cone. Small pink petals will curl inwards and larger flowers curl outwards.

4. Fold all leaves on score lines.

5. Shape all edges of leaves with curling tool.

6. Roll center stamen pieces.

7. Apply glue to base of stamen pieces and place in center of small pink flowers.

8. Thread large needle with green baker's twine. Attach larger flower through center of bloom.

9. Sew through base of leaf to attach to thread.

10. Glue underside of small flower with stamen. Glue leaf to thread and attach flower.

11. Attach third flower and three-pointed leaf cluster by sewing through centers.

12. Attach blue leaves by gluing twine between base of two leaves.

13. Repeat sequence with flowers and leaves to create your paper lei or garland.

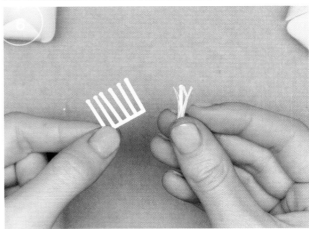

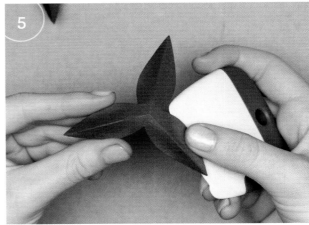

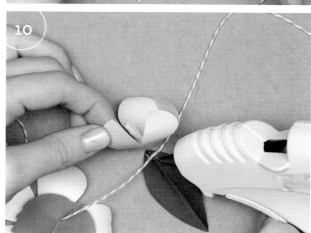

CUPCAKE DECOR

1. Cut leaves from text-weight or card stock paper and use hot glue to attach toothpick.

2. Cut cupcake wrappers from text-weight or card stock paper. Use tab to create wrap shape or glue into position for smaller cupcakes.

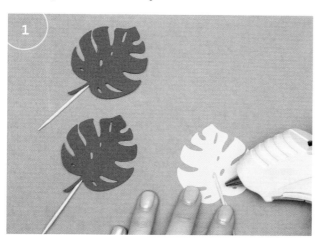

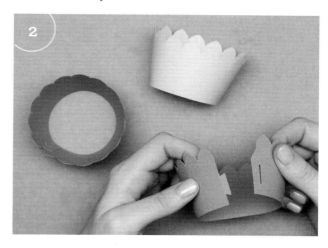

tip: Simply cut the tropical leaves from the files and use them to decorate your table as you see fit.

Ice Cream Stand

Displaying a pretty paper banner transforms a simple scoop into an ice cream social. Add a bit of extra yum with colorful cone wrappers, then sprinkle on the delight! For your ice cream host, make a multicolored customized apron that will keep everyone singing "we all scream for ice cream."

MATERIALS & TOOLS

BANNER AND CONE WRAPS
- text-weight or card stock papers
- pink baker's twine
- double-sided adhesive roller
- large needle
- low-temp hot glue gun

IRON-ON VINYL
- cutting-machine iron-on vinyl
- scissors
- weeding tool
- iron and ironing surface
- smooth cotton ironing cloth

BANNER AND CONE STEPS

1. Cut banner from text-weight or card stock paper.

2. Use double-sided adhesive to secure solid backs onto cut banner fronts.

3. With large needle, attach pieces by inserting pink baker's twine through holes.

4. For cone wraps, cut from text-weight or card stock paper. Shape by gently running paper on edge of table, then secure with hot glue.

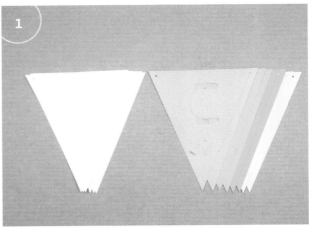

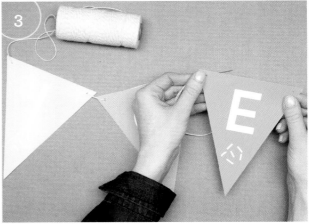

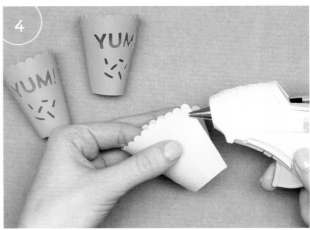

IRON-ON VINYL STEPS

1. Cut all iron-on vinyl pieces with shiny plastic side facing mat and mirroring the cut. Peel excess from designs.

2. Use weeding tool to remove all pieces from details.

3. Position text piece and cone piece onto apron front.

4. With hot iron and no steam, iron into place.

5. Gently remove plastic from design at a sharp angle.

6. One by one, iron layers of ice cream and cherry into place, starting with the bottom and moving up.

tip: Remember to cover your final design with a smooth cotton ironing cloth and give it a final press with the hot iron to secure the design. Do not touch your iron directly onto the exposed iron-on vinyl, as it will melt.

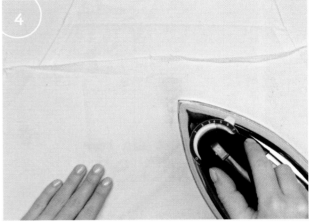

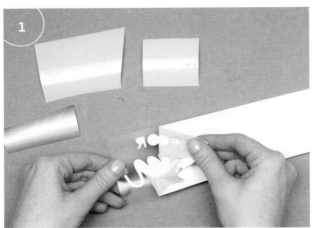

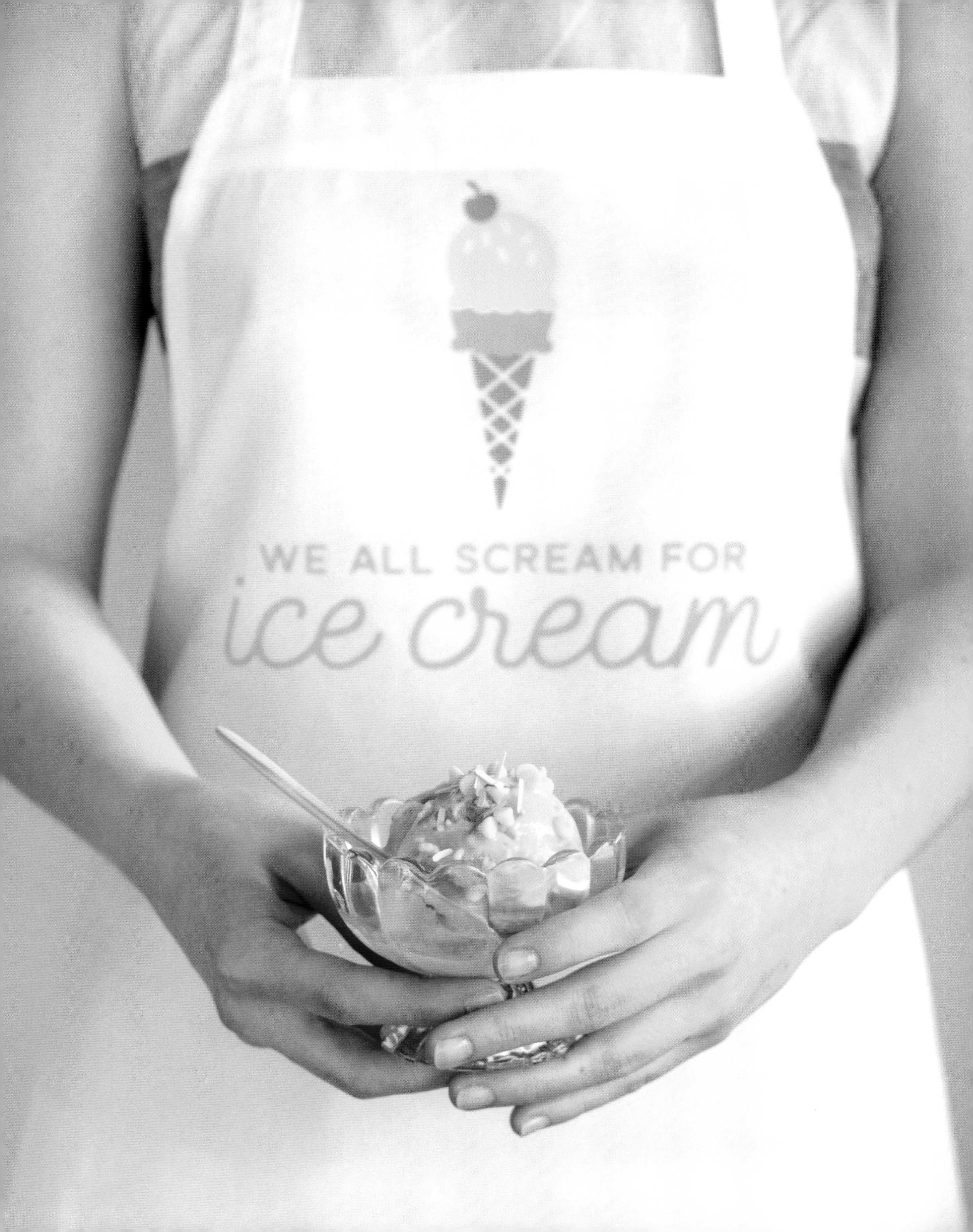
WE ALL SCREAM FOR
ice cream

Spiders and Webs

If you are on the hunt for a frightening party theme, this spooky spider and web combo is a perfect match. The paper spiders become quite real simply by bending their long legs. You can use them to decorate the top of your ghoulish treats or hang them off of the side of your dinner goblets to surely spook your guests. Add a metallic iron-on web to some table linens to complete the look.

MATERIALS & TOOLS

IRON-ON VINYL
- cutting-machine iron-on vinyl
- scissors
- weeding tool
- iron and ironing surface
- smooth cotton ironing cloth
- napkin

PAPER
- text-weight or card stock paper
- low-temp hot glue gun

IRON-ON VINYL STEPS

1. Cut iron-on vinyl web with shiny plastic side facing mat. Peel excess from designs and use weeding tool to remove pieces between web.

2. With scissors, cut your web in half.

3. Postiton web design on the edge of napkin.

4. Use hot iron without steam to infuse vinyl with fabric. Use smooth cotton ironing cloth, if needed.

5. Gently peel back plastic at a sharp angle.

6. Place ironing cloth over design and iron to secure design onto fabric.

tip: Cut large spider webs from white vinyl and add to dark plate. Or simply cut the webs from paper and use them as a removeable layer or under your smaller plates.

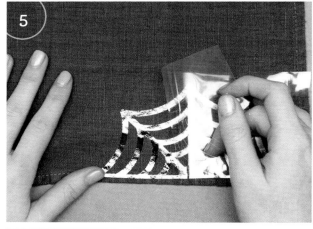

PAPER STEPS

1. For spiders, bend legs at body and joints.

2. For cupcake wraps, use hot glue to attach ends.

3. For napkin rings, use hot glue to create circular form ring.

tip: These pieces can be cut from text-weight or card stock paper. Our favorite is a frosted paper to add shimmer.

Winter Village

The modernity of a white paper village is one of my favorite holiday displays for the fireplace mantle. Mix mini string lights with battery-operated candles between the layers and inside the little houses to add some holiday sparkle.

The houses also make perfect Scandinavian-style ornaments with gold embroidery thread for hanging on the branches. Cut the village design from white vinyl to add a winter theme to glass hurricanes and start dreaming of a white Christmas.

MATERIALS & TOOLS

PAPER
• white card stock paper
• gold embroidery thread
• low-temp hot glue gun

VINYL
• cutting-machine vinyl
• vinyl transfer material
• scissors
• weeding tool
• burnishing tool

PAPER STEPS

1. Cut your village scene from white card stock.

2. Fold along all score lines.

3. Glue tabs and attach pieces of scene.

4. Attach three layers to include mountains, taller buildings, and lower buildings. Make sure all folds create a zigzag that is consistent among all three layers.

5. For small house, cut from white card stock.

6. Fold along all score lines.

7. Glue tab on side of house, and press to secure.

8. For mini lantern, glue top of roof inside house.

9. For ornament, glue top tabs outwards. String gold embroidery thread through hole to hang on tree.

10. Your houses are ready to add lights or hang on the tree.

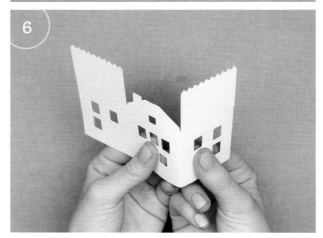

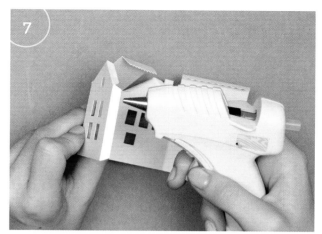

tip: With the same SVG files, cut the middle layer of the file on white vinyl and add to glass hurricane lanterns to create a beautiful wintry effect.

Pink Poinsettias

This chic version of the poinsettia has endeared this winter bloom to me yet again. The pretty frosted pink petals create a gorgeous arrangement mixed with live winter greenery. Add them to a wreath or use one impressive bloom to top your wrapped holiday gifts for that special touch.

MATERIALS & TOOLS

- text-weight or card stock paper
- pale green PanPastel Pigment and brush
- 18-gauge green floral wire
- needle-nose pliers and wire cutters
- low-temp hot glue gun

POINSETTIA STEPS

1. Cut and score poinsettia with text-weight or card stock paper.

2. Fold petals and leaves on score lines.

3. With needle-nose pliers, form spiral at tip of 18-gauge floral wire and bend at a 45-degree angle.

4. Press wire through center of first leaf piece and slide to top.

5. Add hot glue onto wire spiral, then place second leaf piece onto glue. Hold in place until cool.

6. Position and glue first set of petals onto leaf base.

7. Repeat with second and third set of petals, rotating so all petals are evenly spaced.

8. Roll stamen into a spiral.

9. Glue stamen into center of poinsettia.

10. Brush pale green PanPastel Pigment into center of poinsettia petals to add layer of color.

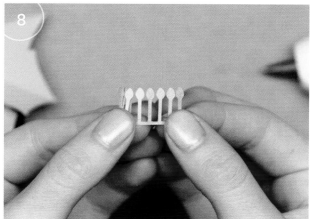

Holiday Evergreens

These paper cut designs are so versatile that you can make quite a variety of projects from the shapes of greenery. Here we show you two versions of wreaths, first the classic and then Scandinavian-inspired mini wreaths. Once you've learned to add shape to the flat paper cuts you'll want to slide a sprig into your holiday napkin rings or surround your display of candles with the colorful conifer.

MATERIALS & TOOLS

- text-weight or card stock paper
- wreath form
- wide green ribbon, for large wreath
- thin ribbon, for mini wreath
- brown paper-wrapped floral wire
- paper curling tool
- needle-nose pliers and wire cutters
- low-temp hot glue gun

EVERGREEN WREATH STEPS

1. Cut pieces from text-weight or card stock paper.

2. Use curling tool to shape fir needles.

3. Curl and shape conifer needles and green pinecones.

4. Gently curl and shape holly berries.

5. Fold holly leaves along all score lines.

6. Fold boxwood leaves in half along score lines.

7. Roll pine needles into a spiral and glue to secure.

8. Shape needles with fingers.

9. Wrap round wreath form with wide green ribbon.

10. In a directional rotation, glue the variety of pieces onto the ribbon-covered wreath.

11. Finish by tucking the last pieces behind the first to complete the wreath.

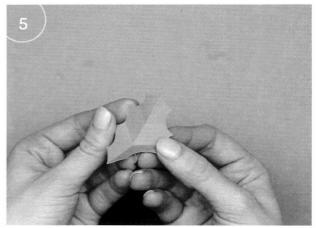

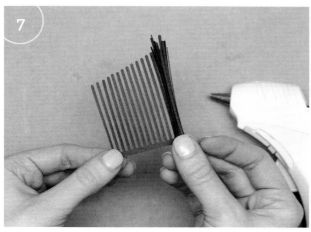

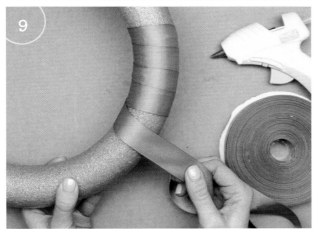

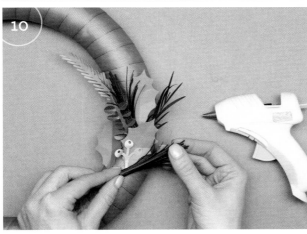

EVERGREEN MINI WREATHS STEPS

1. Form a mini wreath by twisting brown paper–covered floral wire into a circle. Follow steps from large wreath to shape your conifer, fir, and boxwood pieces.

2. Glue conifer needles onto wire wreath, slightly overlapping pieces.

3. Glue fir needles onto wire wreath, slightly overlapping pieces.

4. Glue boxwood leaves onto wire wreath, slightly overlapping pieces.

5. Loop ribbon through wire and tie in double knot.

6. Slide knot to meet wire and add a touch of glue to secure.

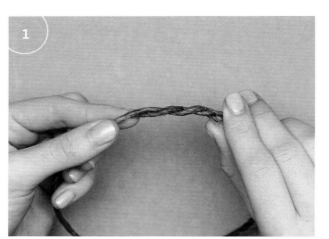

Cozy Season's Greetings

A new set of mix-and-match pillow covers will get you excited to swap them in the last week of November to welcome the winter holidays. Using rose gold foil iron-on vinyl lends a contemporary look to the classic and well-loved sentiments.

MATERIALS & TOOLS

- cutting-machine iron-on vinyl
- pillow covers
- scissors
- weeding tool
- iron and ironing surface
- smooth cotton ironing cloth

SEASON'S GREETINGS STEPS

1. Cut all iron-on vinyl pieces with shiny plastic side facing mat and mirroring the cut.

2. Peel excess from designs.

3. Place design onto center of pillow. With hot iron and no steam, infuse the vinyl with the fabric.

4. Use thin cotton ironing cloth, if needed.

5. Peel plastic layer off at a sharp angle.

6. Place cloth over design and iron to secure the design onto the fabric.

7. Fill pillow with insert.

8. For cleaning, remove insert, wash on gentle cycle and cold temperature, and let air dry.

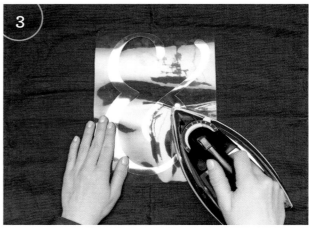

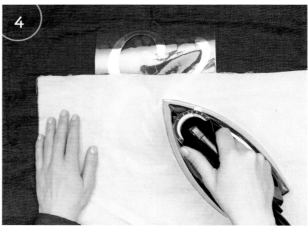

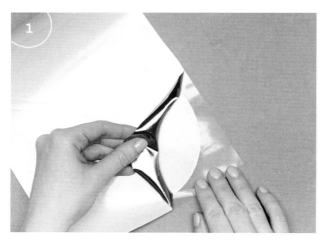

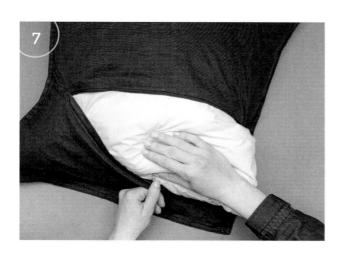

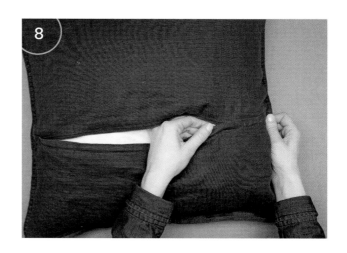

Starry Nights

Our retro-inspired paper stars add a luxe look to holiday decor and are suitable for leaving up long after the New Year's Eve party to brighten the dark nights of winter. We chose a frosted gold paper to add a bit of sparkle and found that the same shape in a flat cut makes a gorgeous garland (see page 183). Enhance tops of your treats or drinks with these mini paper stars or sprinkle them onto your buffet table like confetti.

MATERIALS & TOOLS

- frosted text-weight paper
- low-temp hot glue gun
- gold embroidery thread (for garland)
- removable mounting putty

tip: This project file comes with 3 styles of stars. To make the garland (page 183) tie gold embroidery thread to each star and attach them to a long thread to install on your fireplace mantle or elsewhere. To make the drink decor, hot glue a confetti star to a wooden skewer and pop it into your glass.

STAR STEPS

1. Cut and score shapes using frosted text-weight paper.

2. For star arms, fold on all score lines.

3. Fold towards center to form three-dimensional shapes.

4. Overlap large back tabs and glue into place. Repeat with smaller, angled tabs.

5. Fold large star piece along all score lines.

6. Turn over and overlap flaps, gluing them into place. You will have four arms on your large, center piece.

7. Add hot glue to smaller angled tabs on individual star arms and postion them into place between arms on large, center piece.

8. Position and glue final piece onto back of star. Add mounting putty to back of star for hanging.

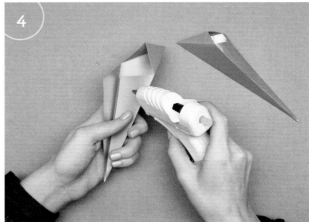

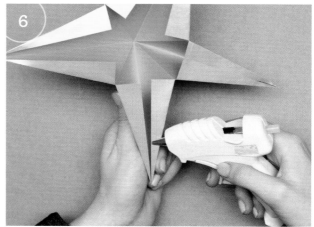

resources

Here's a list of where to find cutting machines, accessories, paper, floral supplies, and more:

Machines and Accessories

AC Moore

Amazon.com

Bed, Bath, and Beyond

Blick Art Materials

CreateandCraft.com (in the UK)

Cricut.com

Hobby Lobby

HSN.com

Jo-Ann

Michaels

QVC.com

Sizzix.com

Silhouette.com

Walmart

Frosted Paper and Art Paper

Blick Art Materials

Liagriffith.com

Paperpapers.com

PanPastel Pigments and Markers

Amazon.com

Blick Art Materials

General Crafting and Floral Supplies

AC Moore

Amazon

Blick Art Materials

Hobby Lobby

Jo-Ann

Michaels

Craft Scissors and Other Tools

Amazon.com

Fiskars.com

Joann.com

Liagriffith.com

Tropical Leaves

PAPER

1 each 12 × 24 Canford art paper: Navy
  Blue and Forest
1 12 × 24 Fabriano art paper: Salvia
PanPastel Pigments: Green Shade,
  Green Tint, and Green
Vases from West Elm

VINYL

1 roll of Cricut vinyl: Foil Matte
  Champagne
Copper tray from Crate & Barrel

IRON-ON

2 rolls of Cricut Iron-On: Foil Rose
  Gold
1 roll of Cricut Iron-On: Charcoal
Pillow from West Elm
Tote from Madewell

Scandinavian Botanicals

VINYL

1 roll each Cricut vinyl: Foil Matte
  Bronze and Foil Matte Gunmetal
Canisters from Crate & Barrel

IRON-ON

1 roll each Cricut Iron-On: Foil
  Pewter, Foil Rose Gold, and Foil
  Light Gold
Linen apron and towels from Crate &
  Barrel

Southwest Cacti

PAPER

4 each 12 × 24 Fabriano art paper:
  Moss Green and Salvia
4 12 × 24 Canford art paper: Forest
1 8.5 × 11 Paper Papers text weight:
  Stardream Coral
3 8.5 × 11 poster board
Terra cotta pots from garden store
  painted slate gray

VINYL

1 each Cricut vinyl: Denim, Silver,
  Olive, Blush, and Mint
Stone coasters from West Elm

Mushroom Meadow

PAPER

1 each 8.5 × 11 Paper Papers text
  weight: Shine Moss, Jelly Bean
  Green, Mohawk Pine, Shine Iron
  Satin, Curious Ink, StardreamCoral
1 12 × 12 Bazzil card stock: Basic
  Thunder
Square frame Ikea Ribba painted slate
  gray

VINYL

1 each Cricut vinyl: Foil Matte
  Champagne and Foil Matte
  Gunmetal
Mugs from Crate & Barrel

Boxwood Greenery

TOPIARY

18 each 8.5 × 11 Paper Papers text
  weight: Shine Moss, Curious Botanic
3 foam balls at 4 inches
Green extra-fine crepe paper

WREATH

18 each 8.5 × 11 Paper Papers text
  weight: Shine Moss, Curious
  Botanic, and Stardream Fairway
12-inch green foam wreath

Gerbera Daisies

QUANTITY

5 each 8.5 × 11 Paper Papers text
  weight: Rose Quartz and Ice Gold
1 each 12 × 12 Cricut Pearl paper:
  Sunshine, Moss, and Forest
4 12 × 12 Cricut Pearl paper: Coral

Meadow Cloche

2 each 8.5 × 11 Paper Papers text
  weight: Mohawk Pine
2 each 8.5 × 11 Paper Source text
  weight: Sage and Paper Bag
Glass cloches from Ikea

Anemone Blossoms

For 12 flowers:

12 8.5 × 11 Paper Papers text weight:
  Curious Ice Gold
2 8.5 × 11 Paper Papers text weight:
  Shine Iron Satin
3 8.5 × 11 Fabriano art paper: Salvia

Paper Lanterns

For 3 large and 3 small lanterns:
3 each 8.5 × 11 Paper Papers text
  weight or card stock: Stardream
  Copper, Curious Ionized, and
  Stardream Bronze
6 8.5 × 11 Paper Papers vellum:
  Platinum
12 Recollections Mini Brads

Centerpiece Succulents

2 each 8.5 × 11 Paper Papers text
  weight: Pure Gold, Aquamarine, and
  Vista
4 8.5 × 11 Paper Papers text weight:
  Spearmint
4 8.5 × 11 Fabriano art paper: Salvia
Terrariums from West Elm
Copper planter from Terrain

Fall Leaves

3 each 8.5 × 11 Paper Papers text
  weight: Pure Gold, Champagne,
  Leaf Green Vellum
15 8.5 × 11 Paper Papers text weight:
  Kraft
3 each 8.5 × 11 Paper Source text
  weight: Sage and Moss
2 8.5 × 11 Fabriano art paper: Polvere
2 8.5 × 11 Canson art paper: Sky Blue

Monster Hugs

IRON-ON

1 roll Siser EasyWeed Heat Transfer
  Vinyl: Mint
1 roll Cricut Iron-On: White
Dress and shirt from Old Navy

PAPER

1 12 × 12 card stock from Cricut: Teal, Seafoam Green, Forest Green, Light Pink. and Rose

Unicorns and Rainbows

IRON-ON

1 roll Cricut Iron-On: White, Blush, White Glitter. and Silver Glitter
Pillow from H&M Home

PAPER

1 each 12 × 12 Recollections card stock: Pink Glitter and Silver Glitter

2 12 × 12 Recollections card stock: Smooth White

1 each 12 × 12 My Mind's Eye card stock: Moonstone Blue, Ballerina Pink, and Lovable

1 each 8.5 × 11 card stock from Paper: Bluebell, and Plum

1 skein each Knit Picks Brava Sport yarn: White, Sky, Blush, and Clanty
Copic Sketch Marker: Rose Quartz
Baker's Twine: Pink

Friendly Insects

PAPER

1 11 × 17 Canford art paper: Barley

1 each 8.5 × 11 Paper Source card stock: Curry, Persimmon, Moss, Chartreuse, Night, and Vellum #30

IRON-ON

1 sheet each Benzie felt: Orange and Moss

1 roll each (need only 4 × 4-inch square) Cricut Iron-On: Sunshine Yellow and Navy

Fairy Crown and Flower Wand

PAPER

1 each 12 × 12 card stock from Recollections: Glitter Paper Rosey

3 yards ¼ inch May Arts silk ribbon: Champagne

1 yard 1.25 inch May Arts silk ribbon: Champagne

Paper Boats

PAPER

1 each 8.5 × 11 Fabriano art paper: Salvia and Moschino; Canson: Indigo Blue

1 each 8.5 × 11 card stock Paper Papers: Brown Paper Bag and SpeckleTone

Forest Friends

PAPER

1 each 8.5 × 11 Paper Source card stock: Moss, Mint, Persimmon, Papaya, Chartreuse, Gravel, Paperbag, and White

IRON-ON

1 roll each Cricut Iron-On: Grey and Sunshine Yellow

Blossom Letters

VINYL

1 roll Cricut Vinyl: White

IRON-ON

1 roll Cricut Iron-On Vinyl: Rose Gold Foil
T-shirt from Old Navy

Love and Hearts

VINYL

1 roll Cricut Vinyl: White and Blush
Apothecary Jars from Sur La Table

PAPER

4 to 5 12 × 12 card stock from Recollections: Glitter Gold

4 to 5 12 × 12 card stock from Cricut: Rose

4 to 5 8.5 × 11 Paper Papers text weight: Rose Quartz, Ice Silver, Antique Gold

Bunnies and Carrots

For 4 bunnies and carrots:

4 8.5 × 11 Paper Papers text weight: Jelly Bean Green

1 8.5 × 11 Paper Papers text weight: Jelly Curious Ionized

4 12 × 12 card stock from Recollections: White Linen

4 12 × 12 card stock from Cricut: Peach

1 skein each Knit Picks Brava yarn: White and Pea Pod
Small pom pom maker
Copic Sketch Marker: Blush

Spring Garden Party

Cake Toppers:

1 each 12 × 12 card stock from Cricut: Sunshine, Moss, Forest, and Coral

1 each 8.5 × 11 Paper Papers text weight: Stardream Rose Quartz and Shine Pearl White

15 to 20 wood toothpicks and thin skewers

5 to 10 gold beads

Backdrop:

10 each 12 × 12 card stock from Cricut: Sunshine, Moss, and Forest

15 each 12 × 12 card stock from Cricut: Coral

10 each 8.5 × 11 Paper Papers text weight: Stardream Rose Quartz and ShinePearl White

1-inch wood beads

3 foot 1" wood dowel

20 feet cotton cord or clothesline

Peony Bouquet

For 7 flowers:

16 8.5 × 11 Paper Papers text weight: Stardream Coral

3 8.5 × 11 Fabriano art paper: Salvia

Tropical Party

PAPER

4 each 8.5 × 11 Paper Papers text weight: Stardream Coral, Pop Tone Pink Lemonade, and Curious Ice Silver

4 8.5 × 11 text weight from Paper Source: Sage

3 12 × 12 Canford art paper: Forest

1 12 × 24 Canford art paper: Indigo Blue

3 12 × 12 Fabriano art paper: Salvia

1 12 × 24 Fabriano art paper: Rosa

Dishes from Crate & Barrel

Napkins from Sur La Table

Ice Cream Stand

PAPER

2 to 4 8.5 × 11 Paper Papers text weight: Pink Lemonade and Whip Cream

2 each 12 × 12 card stock from Cricut: Light Pink, Teal Green, and Peach

IRON-ON

1 roll each Cricut Iron-On: Blush, Carnation, and Gold

1 roll Siser EasyWeed Heat Transfer Vinyl: Mint

Apron from Amazon

Spiders and Webs

PAPER

1 each 8.5 × 11 Paper Papers text weight: Ice Silver and Anthracite

IRON-ON

1 roll each Cricut Iron-On: Foil Pewter

VINYL

1 roll each Cricut Vinyl: White

Gray Plates from H&M Home

Gray Linen from West Elm

Winter Village

PAPER

9 12 × 12 card stock from Recollections: White

DMC Gold Floss

VINYL

1 roll each Cricut Vinyl: White

Paper Wreath is DIY from liagriffith.com

Pink Poinsettia

PAPER

1 each 12 × 24 Canson art paper: Light Green and Forest

4 8.5 × 11 Paper Papers text weight: Stardream Rose Quarz

Paper wreath is DIY from liagriffith.com

Holiday Evergreens

PAPER

1 each 12 × 12 Fabriano art paper: Moss Green

1 each 12 × 12 Fabriano art paper Canson: Green, Indigo Blue

1 each 12 × 12 Bazzill card stock: Avacado

1 8.5 × 11 Paper Papers text weight: Stardream Rose Quarz

Cozy Season's Greetings

IRON-ON

4 rolls of Cricut Iron-On: Rose Gold

Linen pillow covers from H&M Home

Starry Nights

20 8.5 × 11 Paper Papers text weight: Shimmer Pure Gold

1 DMC Diamant Metallic Needlework Thread: Light Gold

acknowledgments

My first book was a whirlwind of a process and a truly collaborative affair. I couldn't have done it without the following people:

The entire Clarkson Potter team, including Amy Boorstein, Derek Gullino, Mia Johnson, Marysarah Quinn, Neil Spitkovsky, Kim Tyner, Merri Ann Morrell, and Alison Hagge.

Angelin Borsics, for the insight and creativity needed to plan, organize, and edit this book. Doris Cooper and Aaron Wehner, for their support of the project from the beginning. And Erica Gelbard, for pitching the book to the press and helping to bring it to the public.

Lindsay Zogas, Krista Nuro, Jessica Nash and Meagan, for their clever designs and craftiness in creating all of the projects for these pages.

Brian MacDonnell, for gorgeous photography and Anna Sjoberg-Smith for helping me to style all of the photos and keeping us on schedule.

Emily Criswell, Jessica Nash, and Matthew Nash, for the photo tutorials.

Deanna Washington, for organizing the project, photo editing, and being my right hand.

And to all of the models who beautifully showcased the cutting machine projects.